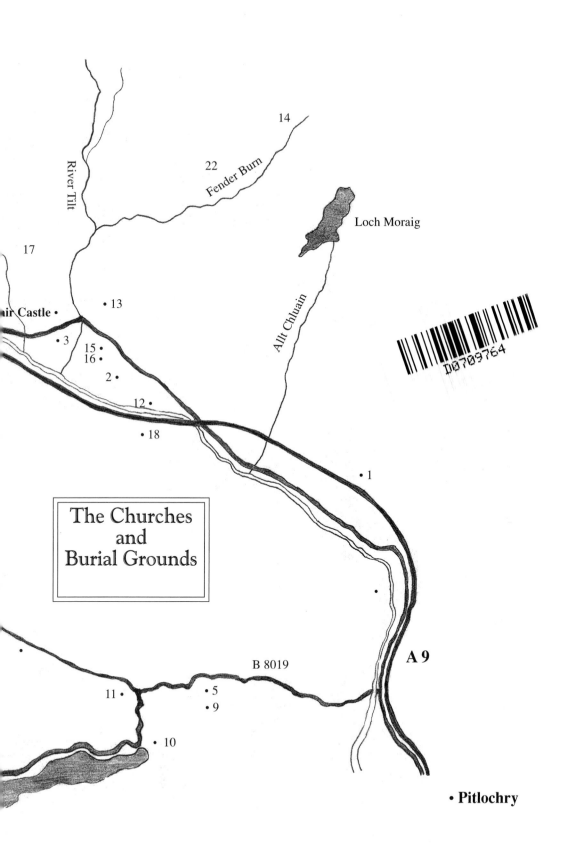

The Churches
and
Burial Grounds

14

22   Fender Burn

Loch Moraig

River Tilt

17

ir Castle •   • 13

Allt Chluain

• 3

15 •
16 •

2 •

12 •

• 18

• 1

B 8019

A 9

11 •   • 5

• 9

• 10

• Pitlochry

D0709764

Church
and
Social History
of Atholl

Church

and

Social History

of Atholl

John Kerr

Foreword by the Very Reverend Sir Robin Barbour

Perth & Kinross Libraries

This book is dedicated to three of my grandchildren
Ioni, Jacob and Dominic

The Publisher is grateful for a subsidy from the Blair Charitable Trust towards the publication of this book.

ISBN 0 905452 25 9

Published by Perth & Kinross Libraries
A K Bell Library, 2-8 York Place, Perth, PH2 8EP

Photography John Kerr

Printed by Cordfall Ltd. 0141 332 4640

Front Cover: Trinafour Church

Contents

Foreword
Robin Barbour, Glen Fincastle

The life of the Church has through the centuries been of enormous importance to the people of Scotland; and in many ways it still is. So John Kerr has done a great service to us in Atholl by bringing together a great deal of the available information about the Church in these parts, and especially about its buildings, its ministers and its elders in the last three hundred years. It will interest us all to discover how many people there were in the various districts of Atholl – and how sparse the provision of church buildings and ministers often was until about a hundred years ago. We can find out in John Kerr's pages how there were indeed disputes and differences of opinion as well as much goodwill among the lairds and folk of importance, but that on the whole it was a very uniform society; we can learn much about how the affairs of the Kirk were managed, and he has wisely included a lot of detail about the actual buildings, which gives an interesting insight into the techniques and costs of building in the 18th and 19th centuries. That will be of interest outside the circle of those who want to know about church affairs.

John Kerr's other publications have shown him to be an assiduous and careful researcher who has contributed enormously to the study of the history of Atholl. This book will enhance his reputation further.

Robin Barbour
May 1998

Introduction

In pre-Reformation times there were five parishes in the Atholl area, each acknowledging Rome as its head. Three of these – Lude, Kilmaveonaig and Struan had close associations with the Robertsons of Clan Donnachaidh, while St Brides, and to a lesser extent, Fincastle, had Stewart connections. Sometime after 1560 Fincastle was joined with Dull parish, while the other four combined to form a parish which covered some five hundred square miles of mainly mountainous terrain.

The antiquity of the religious sites in Atholl is apparent from the survival of the names of the saints connected with their foundation. Kilmaveonaig was consecrated in the name of St Adamnan or possibly St Beoghna, both abbots in Iona in the seventh century, while the church in Old Blair was dedicated to St Bride who died in 525 AD. Struan church was originally named after St Fillan, whose name lingered on for many centuries in a nearby healing well and annual market.

The Robertsons of Lude were staunch supporters of the House of Stuart which could account for Kilmaveonaig retaining an episcopalian form of worship from the time of the Reformation and on through the Jacobite political and religious upheavals of the seventeenth and eighteenth centuries. Both Struan and St Brides adopted presbyterian worship after the Reformation and were extensively repaired in 1723 and 1742. The tradesmen's estimates submitted to Dunkeld Presbytery provide a great deal of information about the former Struan church, indicating its size, details of doors and windows and that it was a "dark, ill-lit place". The cost of these repairs was borne by the local heritors, their proportions being based on the value of the rents paid by their tenants and the largest individual landowner was the Duke of Atholl who paid 63% of the total. By the early 1800s Struan church was very dilapidated and after the failure of attempts to close it, a new one was built. Before this happened, the minister and kirk session completed an extensive questionnaire which is reproduced in full. The form, complete with answers provides a fascinating insight into the make-up of the parish in the 1800s.

Profiles of the family connections of many of the ministers and where they came from since the seventeenth century give us some insight into them as people. Duncan Stewart "intruded" into the parish, having become friendly with the 1st duke who withdrew his support in 1715 because of Stewart's Jacobite affiliations. James MacLagan compiled the parish details for the first Statistical Account in 1792 and seems to have spent much time persuading heritors to provide meal for the poor. The opening of St Brides vault in 1864 was witnessed by the Reverend Dr Alexander Irvine who included details of the findings in his *History of the Church at Old Blair*.

A chapter is devoted to the attempted closure of Struan church in the 1820s, instigated by the minister, John Stewart, and actively supported by the 4th Duke of Atholl who maintained it would be better to have one church to serve the parish. The Robertson heritors vigorously opposed this move and parish opinion was split. The arguments intensified and the anger and dismay of various Robertson heritors is revealed in correspondence of the time. Finally, the question of closure came before the Lords of Council and Session, the highest church court in Scotland, who decreed that not only should Struan remain as a place of worship but that a new church should be built.

St Brides was also repaired in the 1820s but within two years the old military road through "Blair Town" was closed and a new route opened through the Haugh of Blair with the completion of the new Tilt bridge. A new church, capable of holding six hundred people, was built beside this road in 1825, when once again "valued rents" were applied to allocate construction costs and seat allocations were worked out by a county sheriff and the duke's lawyer.

The various manses and glebes have been researched, including St Brides manse, which ceased to be inhabited nearly two hundred and fifty years ago and has now completely disappeared. However, estimates for repairs in 1727 and 1742 tell us much about the building. In 1750 it was replaced by a completely new manse two miles to the west at Baluain and again tradesmen's estimates give a good idea of the building and its rooms. This building has also completely gone and its exact location is not clear. It was replaced by another manse built nearby in 1826 and this is now a private house called "The Old Manse".

As early as 1710 the need for another church was raised for people living miles away from St Brides in the east and south of the parish but it was 1836 before a Chapel of Ease was built at Tenandry. Presbytery minutes reveal its planning and constitution with details of the area to be included and the population of each settlement.

In the 1840s the newly-formed Free Church attracted a large following and not surprisingly, opposition from many of the heritors who were determined to eradicate its presence. Only through determination and holding services in the open air did the movement survive. Following the erection of a wooden church in King's Island, more permanent places of worship gradually followed, at St Andrews church in Bridge of Tilt and at Clachan of Struan.

The history of churches in Atholl is closely linked with the social history of the people of the parish. The kirk session was the local court overseeing morality and good conduct of the parishioners and defaulters were required to "compear" before the session to account for themselves and be judged and punished accordingly. *Church and Social History of Atholl* is based on original research from documents held mainly in Blair Castle archives and the Scottish Record Office. These first-hand records give an insight into life in the parish across hundreds of years – the noise of history is all around us, largely undisturbed.

John Kerr
Old Struan

Acknowledgements

Many people have given me help towards the writing of *Church and Social History of Atholl*. Sir Robin Barbour gave me access to the Tenandry kirk session minutes and provided information about burial grounds in his neighbourhood. Lady Margaret Barbour, author of *A Short History of Tenandry Kirk 1836-1986* has kindly allowed me to use extracts from it, including a seating plan. The Reverend Roger Devonshire was helpful in making available Kilmaveonaig records from Holy Trinity in Pitlochry and Lavinia Gordon, Lude also provided more material on that church. The Reverend James Weatherhead, at 121 George Street, Edinburgh, made his extensive library available to me and provided most useful background material on Established and Free churches.

John Cameron, Monzie, has provided me with information from his Country Collection archive, which I much appreciate. Sebastian Thewes, Strathgarry House, provided access to the Strathgarry papers concerning the formation of Tenandry parish and the nearby Stewart burial ground. Donald Mackinlay, Trinafour, kindly opened up Trinafour church for me and helped decipher the inscription on the bell.

I have included an extract about worship in the farmhouse at Kirkton of Lude, Glenfender, from notes kindly supplied by Kitty Patterson, St Andrews. James Irvine Robertson, Aberfeldy, generously gave me copies of heritors' letters from the time of the attempted suppression of Struan church and also correspondence of his ancestor, the Reverend Dr Alexander Robertson Irvine, from the period of the Disruption at Tenandry. My thanks are also due to the Scottish Record office, particularly to Hugh Scanlon, for his invaluable assistance in supplying the Dunkeld Presbytery minutes and also the session and deacon minutes of the Free Church. As always, in everything I write about Atholl, I acknowledge with gratitude the continuing assistance I receive from Jane Anderson, archivist, Blair Castle, in locating even the most obscure material. Finally, to all those who have in any way helped me in this project, I give my sincere thanks.

Abbreviations

AC	Atholl Chartularies
BCCR	Blair Castle Charter Room
CAT	Chronicles of the Atholl & Tullibardine Families 1908, 1991
CDA	Clan Donnachaidh Annual
DPD	Diocese and Presbytery of Dunkeld 1660-1689
Fasti	Fasti Ecclesiae Scoticanae
JIR	James Irvine Robertson
PSAS	Proceedings of the Society of Antiquaries of Scotland
SHS	Scottish History Society
SRO	Scottish Record Office
TGSI	Transactions of the Gaelic Society of Inverness
TKSM	Tenandry Kirk Session Minutes

one

The Reformation

According to the 1792 Statistical Account for the parish of Blair Atholl and Struan, written by the minister, the Rev James MacLagan:

> These parishes commonly go by the name of the united parishes of Blair-Atholl and Strowan. They consisted formerly of the parishes of Blair-Atholl, Strowan, Lude and Kilmaveonog. . . . These united parishes are situated in the shire of Perth, in the presbytery of Dunkeld, and the synod of Perth and Stirling. Their extent is upwards of 30 miles in length; and, allowing for the ascents and descents of the hills, above 18 miles in breadth. Through a large tract of country, the surface and appearances are various. On the summits of the high mountains, the weather has left little else than gravel and stones, covered with moss.

The combined parish lies half way between Inverness and Edinburgh and is situated in the north-west corner of Highland Perthshire. It covers some five hundred square miles, from Loch Tummel in the south to the county boundaries of Aberdeenshire and Inverness-shire in the north and from the Pass of Drumochter in the north-west to the hamlet of Aldclune in the south-east.

Parsonage in Bagimond
Until 1560, the four parishes acknowledged Rome as their head and paid their tithes there. These parishes were parsonages in the Bagimond Rolls, a statement of accounts in which Baiamund de Vicia collected a tithe called "Peter's Pence" from the parishes of Scottish churches in 1275 to fund the Crusades for the relief of the Holy Land. The fact that these four parishes are featured in these Rolls show they were of some importance and in existence before 1275. In an account of receipts and expenses by Sir Thomas Greg, Canon of Dunkeld, for the period 22 April 1505 to 4 January 1506, it was shown that twelve merks were paid to Rome, with St Brides and Struan each paying four merks, while Kilmaveonaig and Lude each paid two.[1] A Scots merk was a silver coin worth thirteen shillings and four pence (67p).

Each parish had a congregation based on its own geographical area which was as follows: **Lude** parish took in all settlements on the north side of Glenfender, also the Monzies and Shinagags, Dalginross and the Campsies on the east side of Glen Tilt. **Kilmaveonaig** parish, to the east of the River Tilt, contained everything south of the Fender Water to the River Garry and included Strathgroy and settlements north of Aldclune. **Struan** parish covered the whole of Glen Errochty, the Bohespics, the Invervack settlements and Glen Garry as far south as Bruar Water. **St Brides** parish included everything west and north from the Tilt to the Bruar and all settlements south of the

River Garry, excepting Strathgarry and Shierglas, as far as the north shore of Loch Tummel. **Fincastle**, a fifth parish, of which little is known, took in the glen and adjacent parts of Strathtummel and was united with the parish of Dull early in the seventeenth century.[2]

Early Priests and Ministers
Very little has been recorded about the early priests and ministers in the area. Sir John Martyn, born in Dunkeld, had the charge of Lude church in 1514 and was a capable musician, having taken part since his youth in church services and running a choir. Walter Leslie, commissary general of the see of Dunkeld, was succeeded by John Mathlyson to the charge of St Brides in 1546. He built a vicarage "for the salvation of his own soul and of souls in the place" as well as erecting a stone enclosure for growing vegetables. He is reputed to have kept a comfortable house and to have been generous to the poor with food and money.[3] Leonard Leslie was at St Brides at the time of the Reformation and by 1574, John Bartane was the minister in charge of six parishes. He was paid £89.6.8 Scots and to assist him, a reader was appointed to each parish as follows: John Neillis, Cluny; John Leslie, Kilmaveonaig; Alex Stewart and Thomas Cameron, Blair Atholl; Duncan Robertson, Struan; George Mackintosh, Lude and Patrick Williamson, Rannoch. Readers were paid £16 Scots plus victuals to augment their income, except Duncan Robertson who received £14.7.9 and Patrick Williamson who was paid twenty merks.[4] Up until 1572, a reader was permitted only to read prayers and texts from the Bible, after which time he had authority to officiate at baptisms and marriages.

In the accounts of the *Thirds of Benefices* we find the following annual charges applying between 1561 and 1572:[5]

Parsonage and Vicarage of Blair in Atholl	£22.4.5
Strowane	£14.17.9
Kilmaveynok	£22.4.5
Luid	£14.17.9

By 1585 Duncan McCawley was minister in charge of Inchaddin (Kenmore), Fothergill (Fortingall), Kilmaveonaig, Blair Atholl, Struan and Lude. The presbytery of Dunkeld was constituted between October 1581 and April 1582 and the three presbyteries of Dunkeld, Perth and Dunblane were formed into a synod shortly after.[6]

Writing about his parish in 1820, the Reverend John Stewart observed:

The parish of Blair Atholl consists of four united parishes viz: Blair, Lude, Strowan and Kilmaveonaig. At what period these parishes were united is uncertain. Lude and Kilmaveonaig are to the east of Blair and Strowan to the West. The church at Blair was made the parish church, and where the manse and parochial school were situated. It is probable that at the date of the annexation the churches of Lude and Kilmaveonaig were ruinous and that as the church of Strowan happened to be in good repair, it was retained as a place of public worship and in which the minister has continued to preach every third Sunday.[7]

However, there were other reasons why Struan church was retained as a place of worship and these appear in a memorandum prepared for the Duke of Atholl:

8 June 1820

... It may be remarked that although when the parishes of Blair and Strowan were originally annexed, the intervention of the rapid and dangerous Garry betwixt Strowan and Blair Atholl formed a very sufficient reason for keeping up the church of Strowan, that reason no longer exists. The date of the annexation cannot be discovered but it must have been at a very remote period, and until within these few years there was no communication betwixt the parishes unless by Ferries or a circuit of 30 or 40 miles by the head of Loch Garry. There is now however an excellent bridge built near where the church of Strowan stands, at the junction of the Garry and Errochty. Before the bridge was built, it is not surprising that it should have been considered more convenient for the minister alone to ferry over the Garry once in three weeks, than the whole congregation of Strowan to do so weekly, to attend worship at Blair Atholl church. Because of this obstacle as well as the smallness of the Blair Atholl church, many of the inhabitants of Bohespick and Strathtummel were obliged to purchase seats in Strowan church. [8]

After the Reformation, celebration of the Latin mass was forbidden and Scotland adopted presbyterianism. In the years between 1575 and 1690, contention whether presbyterian or episcopalian forms of worship should be followed, alternated between one system of church order and the other. First one and then the other obtained a temporary ascendancy and in this situation sometimes every parish church was episcopalian and then presbyterian. In 1584 they were episcopalian, 1592 presbyterian, 1610 back to episcopalian, 1638 presbyterian, 1661 episcopalian again and finally presbyterian in 1690.[9]

"Covenanters", namely those who had fought for religious practice to be independent of state control, saw this principle become the basis of a new system after the flight of the catholic King James II and VII to France in 1688:

On 25 April 1690, Parliament met and gave us the church as we enjoy it today; and measures were ever more significant than those that were passed. Presbyterian ministers were restored in their livings. The government of the church was again in the courts of the kirk sessions, presbyteries, synods, and general assemblies. The General Assembly agreed that Episcopal clergymen could retain their livings upon condition that they acknowledged Presbyterian church government and took the oath of King William.[10]

After 1690 episcopacy retained considerable support in Highland Perthshire, particularly in Atholl where attempts to oust ministers were resisted. On 31 May 1706 the Duke of Atholl observed:

I have always allowed the churches where I am concerned when they are vaccant to be planted by Presbyterian ministers, but have also thought it just and reasonable to preserve the Episcopal ministers who are good men in the churches they possess.[11]

Early Church Architecture

At the end of the seventeenth century church architecture in general was not of a high order and in rural areas the buildings were generally mean and poor. The simplicity which characterised presbyterianism often resulted in a church of four walls with a thatched roof and a bell hanging from a nearby tree. A puritanical spirit had so taken hold of the Scottish mind that it was assumed that discomfort increased spirituality in worship. There was no proper flooring in these buildings, usually just beaten earth and they were empty of furniture with the congregation standing for the service, or sitting on stools or chairs which they brought for their own use. The placing of removable seats led to quarrels, when one man would move another's, replacing it with his own. Later, when heritors began putting in "desks" for themselves, rough flagstones were sometimes laid along the aisles and boards placed for feet to rest on.

Church buildings tended to be long, narrow and low with the door and windows in the south wall and occasionally a window in the east or west gables but none in the north wall. Windows were few and small and the church interiors must have been very dark and ill-lit. Later, the pulpit was generally placed in the middle of the south wall with galleries running along the east and west sides and sometimes on the north, in front of the minister. Part of the gallery was often called the "Common Loft" where those to whom no specified space was allocated, generally sat.[12]

A description of "the situation of some Highland Parishes above Dunkeld by the Presbytery of Dunkeld" in 1716 runs as follows:

> The paroch of Blair Atholl and Strowan, from the head of Glen Tilt to Bohespick is 15 or 16 miles in length and has interjected a great part of the Parish of Dull viz: Shierglas, Pitdornie, Bonscood, and Glen of Fincastle, as also a part of the parish of Muline lying within a mile and a half of the church of Blair viz. the lands of Strathgarrie. It hath two places of worship, Blair Atholl and Struan, at three miles distance, with the Water of Struan interveening.[13]

Writing to the Duke of Atholl in 1734, the Reverend Alex Stoddard of Falkland parish observed that "the Act of Patronage of 1712 was galling to many presbyterians" and had resulted in some of the clergy "who have no oye [other] means of making themselves considerable, to cry up the power and right of the people to elect their own Pastors which is the principall and only ground of our Assembly of 1732". This Assembly had established that the procedures of the 1690 act should be followed, whereby ministers were called by heritors and elders in parishes where the patron "does not exercise his right within a time limit".[14] Apparently "wilde" ministers had complained about this and their charges were declared vacant. This resulted in some ministers setting up their own charges.

In 1820, Dr Alexander Niven, clerk of the Presbytery of Dunkeld, described the state of the parish as follows:

> The Churches of Little Lude and Kilmaveonaig are gone. The glebe remains upon the seite of Kilmaveonaig where an Episcopal Church is built. It is the representation of the former parish church. By accident two of the former parish churches remain. . . . No alterations upon either since the Reformation. It is a matter of notoriety that the miserable looking places called churches at Blair and Struan have been in that miserable state for at least half a century.[15]

Population
According to Dr Webster's 1755 survey of the population of the parish, there were 3,257 inhabitants. In August 1791 the figure had dropped slightly to 3,120 people, made up of 1,480 males and 1,640 females, of which total nearly 25% were children under the age of eight.[16] By 1814 the number had declined to 2,333

and according to a census carried out by the elders in 1836, numbers had dropped to 2,312 people living in the parish.[17] Dr Niven, clerk to the Dunkeld presbytery, accounted for this 30% drop in under a hundred years, when he wrote:

> There have been in the course of these last forty years, great changes in the State of the population in the United Parishes. In some once populous districts the people have completely disappeared. They have been obliged to obey the mandate "veteres migrati coloni" [ancestors migrating to the colonies]. The population has upon the whole diminished greatly and within these few years a considerable change has taken place.[18]

In the 1961 census the population was recorded as 1,458 people.

References

1. SHS *Rentale Dunkeldense*
2. *Fasti,* Scott
3. SHS *Rentale Dunkeldense*
4. *Wodrow Society Miscellany*
5. SHS *Thirds of Benefices*
6. DPD, Hunter
7. BCCR Trunk 33 XVIII
8. Ibid
9. *Scotland, Church and Nation,* Donaldson
10. *The Wood Burns Away...* Rees
11. *Living in Atholl,* Leneman
12. New Spalding Club 1897
13. SRO CH 2 106/3
14. BCCR Trunk 46 (8) 7
15. BCCR Trunk 33 XVIII
16. *Statistical Account* 1792
17. *New Statistical Account* 1843
18. BCCR Trunk 33 XVIII

Extract from "A General Map of Scotland and Islands" by James Dorret, 1750, showing the parish.

The parish boundary beside the railway at Drumochter. Asa Pinney was herding a flock of sheep from Queensferry to Thurso for a TV programme.

two

Combined Parish Boundary

The origins of a parish can be traced back almost to the dawn of written history. Though parishes were not part of the organisation of the Celtic church, they have their origins in the geographical distribution of the missions of that church. When feudalism was established in the early twelfth century, the territories of the clan or local landowner generally subdivided the country into parishes, which by the middle of that century, had formalised into districts. These remained largely intact until the time of the Reformation and with minor alterations, until the present day.[1]

Sometime after the Reformation, the four parishes were united to form the combined parish of Blair Atholl and Struan, with a boundary of about a hundred miles in length. Starting at the confluence of the Garry and Tummel rivers at the foot of the Pass of Killiecrankie, the boundary follows the Tummel westwards through the Linn of Tummel, a well-known beauty spot, amongst whose famous visitors were Queen Victoria and Prince Albert in 1844.

Dull Parish

Below Bonskeid House the boundary met the civil parish of Dull, and, under section 49 of the 1889 Local Government (Scotland) Act, that part of Dull parish, north of the Tummel loch and river, was transferred to Blair Atholl.[2] Under the heading "Paroch of Dull" this area was described in 1700 as follows:

Boundary stone on the parish march, south of Loch Garry.

> In Atholl beyond ye Water of Timbell a long tract of a country divided from Apnadull by huge and vast mountains from Glen of Foncastle Bonscood and Sierglas all environs and Sierglas being in view of and almost within a gun shot of Blair.[3]

This area included the estates of Bonskeid, Allean, Bohally and Dalcroy on Tummelside, Fincastle in its own glen and Shierglas, Pitdornie and Tombeithe, part of Atholl estate, on the south side of the River Garry.

From the river, the line goes straight through the middle of Loch Tummel, on past Tummel Bridge, built by General Wade's troops in 1730 to take his military road southwards out of

23

Atholl. A mile further upstream it leaves the river and crosses open countryside in a north-westerly direction. Here the boundary is man-made, following a series of dykes which run uphill and then descend into Loch Errochty. Then the march turns due west, retracing the submerged route formerly taken by the Feachory Water, the stream that flowed down the glen before it was dammed. The land at the west end of the loch was ground held in common by the parishes of Blair Atholl, Fortingall and Logierait but under the provisions of the 1889 Boundary Act, that part north of Allt Sliebh was transferred to Blair Atholl, with the burn forming the new march.[4]

For the next two miles the boundary is unmarked and proceeds in a straight line across flat, featureless terrain to a conspicuous little knoll where it changes direction and this point is marked by a tiny cairn, marked as "pile of stones" on the 1900 Ordnance Survey six inch map. Within a few hundred yards it reverts to natural features, following Allt Shallainn to Loch Garry, when it turns sharply westwards, climbing Allt Coire Easan to reach the watershed at the head of Coire Dhomhain, on a hill called Carn 'Ic Loumhaidh.

The railway viaduct through the Pass of Killiecrankie, here pictured in 1870, ran beside the parish boundary.

County Boundary

This watershed marks the county boundary between Perthshire and Inverness-shire and the parish boundary follows it for several miles, across Beinn Udlamain and An Torc, more commonly known as the Boar of Badenoch, before descending to the Drumochter Pass. Here the boundary is clearly marked by a post and wire fence running down to the railway, which at this point, at 1,484 feet (457m), is the highest reached by a railway line anywhere in Britain. Drumochter, the great pass through the Grampian Mountains, was described as follows in an 1843 guide book:

The black and moorish wilds where nought but stunted grass and heather, dark swamp, impetuous torrents, grey rocks and frowning heights and precipices are to be seen. The mountains also are heavy and seem to be broken into great detached mounds.[5]

The old Killiecrankie bridge built in the 1770s across the Garry following a ferry disaster, spanned the parish march.

The parish boundary now follows the county march for nearly forty miles across some of the most rugged and desolate countryside in the Highlands. After about ten miles it crosses Vinegar Hill and descends steeply to Loch an Duin where it is marked by a stone dyke with a gateway across the track from Dalnacardoch to Gaick. After crossing the thirteenth century Comyn's Road at Bac na Creige and the seventeenth century Minigaig Pass at Coire Bhran, it reaches Carn an Fhidleir, the Fiddler's Cairn, which marks the meeting point, on a 3,000 feet (923 m) ridge, of the three counties of Perthshire, Inverness-shire and Aberdeenshire. Three miles to the east, the march crosses An Sgarsoch, the mountain on which an ancient cattle and horse market is reputed to have been held. Traces of a stone causeway were said to be visible near the summit in the nineteenth century.[6] Continuing eastwards the boundary passes round Loch Tilt, described by Thomas Pennant in 1769 as "a small piece of water, swarming with trouts" from whence the boundary goes on to cross the Tilt watershed at a height of 1,500 feet (462 m).

After a further ten miles the march leaves the county boundary on the ridge of Mam nan Carn beside Loch nan Eun and heads south-east to cross the Glen Fernate watershed, the Seven Shielings area and the land of Lude, by following natural features such as ridges, peaks and rivers. South of Shinagag the parish boundary took in Reinakyllich, whose lands, bounded by Allt Girnaig to the west, Shinagag to the north, Cornacraig to the east and Urrard to the south, were transferred to the parish of Moulin in 1889.[7] After this, the boundary follows a line from Allt nam Breac, Allt Dubhag and Allt Girnaig for a short distance before branching off to the west, heading for Allt Chluain. This it follows downstream to reach the hamlet of Aldclune and the north bank of the River Garry above the Killiecrankie gorge.

The fourth alteration relating to the Blair Atholl boundary in 1889 concerned Strathgarry, which at that time was part of Moulin parish. This estate, consisting of some 259 acres with a mansion house, was transferred to Blair Atholl.[8]

The boundary follows the River Garry down through the Pass of Killiecrankie, below the Soldier's Leap and the railway viaduct, opened by the Perth and Inverness Junction Railway Company in 1863. Until forty years or so ago, a fine, arched stone bridge, which was built in the 1770s following a ferry disaster in which eighteen people drowned, straddled the river carrying the road to Tummelside and Rannoch. It was replaced further down river in the 1970s by the present bridge. Just below it, the parish boundary emerges from the steep-sided, tree-clad gorge to complete the hundred mile circuit at the meeting place of the two rivers.

References

1. TGSI Volume XXXVIII
2. *Boundaries of Counties and Parishes in Scotland,* Shennan
3. BCCR Trunk 29 I (7) 126
4. *Boundaries of Counties and Parishes in Scotland,* Shennan,
5. *Guide to the Highlands,* Anderson
6. TGSI Volume LIV
7. *Boundaries of Counties and Parishes in Scotland,* Shennan,
8. Ibid

three

Lude Church
Glenfender

The ruins of the ancient church of Lude are to be found a few miles up Glenfender, on a level piece of ground on the west bank of the Fender Water. It is difficult to be precise about the date of the final closure of this church, which was in the heartland of the lands of the Robertsons of Lude and was a parish with strong Clan Donnachaidh connections. The first main dwelling house of the Robertson of Lude family lay somewhere nearby, although searches both from the ground and air have failed to reveal traces of it. An indication of its location comes from a nineteenth century map[1] which shows Lude House opposite the church on the east side of the river. It is possible that it was near or under the buildings of Monzie Farm, the principal holding of the estate. Its situation is strategic, with commanding views of the whole area and is documented as having a close association with the Robertson family from the fifteenth century.

The clue to the Gaelic derivation of "Lude" may come from the slope on which the old house stood, as *leathad* means a broad slope of hillside which could be ploughed in one direction only. The old house was burnt down by Cromwellian troops in the 1650s as punishment for the Robertson support of the Stuart cause and thereafter the family moved house down the glen to Balnagrew,

The old Lude church showing the east gable before it was taken down for safety reasons.

above Bridge of Tilt, the site of the present Lude House. It is probable that this move coincided with the closure of Lude church as a place of worship.

Tradition tells us that local Jacobites called out in 1745 by Lord George Murray, buried their valuables in the aisle of the church before they left the glen but despite a number of digs over the years, nothing has ever been found.[2]

Glebe

An early nineteenth century map[3] shows the presence of a triangular-shaped glebe which was detached from the main part a few hundred yards downstream. Agreement was reached in 1794 between James Robertson of Lude and the Reverend James MacLagan "for the right and privilege of a cart road from the main part of the Glebe of Lude to the detached part thereof".[4] The main glebe was adjacent to the churchyard and measured 5.75 acres. Glebes were leased out to the highest bidder and in 1794 the rent was £12.12.0. By 1815 this had dropped to £8.0.6, a figure made up of one acre of pastureland at eighteen shillings an acre and 4.75 acres of arable ground at thirty shillings an acre. By 1834 the amount had increased to £10.10.0.[5]

Kirkton Glebe, a settlement in the north-west corner of the glebeland, was home to three families comprising fifteen people in 1841. Kirkton of Lude, appearing as Balnaheglish in a map of 1780,[6] was a large settlement just outside the glebe, which in 1723 paid a rent of £80 Scots and casualties of a stone of butter and cheese, a wedder, hogg and 12 poultry. In the early part of the twentieth century, a service was held once a month in the sitting room of the house. The services were conducted by the Reverend Hugh MacCallum, the United Free Church minister for Blair Atholl and Struan. He was inducted on 8 October

Part of "Plan of the Common of Glentilt as divided" by David Buist, 1808, showing the old Lude church, surrounding settlements and the detached glebe.

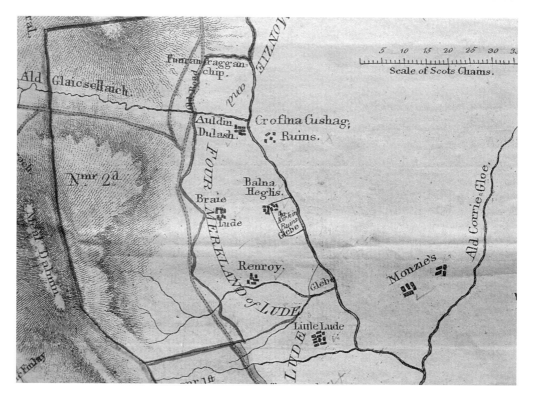

1903, having transferred from Tummel Bridge and he died on 19 April 1920. The services were always well attended and the congregation "sang hymns and was very religious".[7]

According to a report in 1830, the walls of the church were still largely intact but the roof had entirely gone. Considerable deterioration took place over the following century as was confirmed in a report by the archaeological department of the Scottish Ordnance Survey in the 1950s:

> The walls of the church are still standing. Lude was a separate parish at some time before 1632. The remains of this church consist of a nave 9.0 m long and 6.0 m wide and a chancel 5.0 m long and 4.8 m wide. The walls of the chancel are about 1 m high and much obscured by debris. The walls of the nave stand generally to roof height about 3.0 m high, the east gable being almost entire.

Since then further deterioration has occurred but in 1990, to preserve and stabilise the remaining structure, Major W. Gordon, the current owner of Lude estate, took down the precariously unstable east gable for safety reasons, cleared the interior of debris, had the tops of the walls cemented to prevent further erosion and erected a wrought-iron gate in the doorway to keep out livestock. From time to time a service is held beside the ruin in midsummer to commemorate its former use as a hallowed place of worship.

A midsummer service outside the old Lude church.

References

1. *Comitatus de Atholia*, Robertson
2. Mrs K. Patterson
3. Plan of the Common of Glentilt, Buist 1808
4. BCCR Trunk 9 V 6
5. BCCR Bundle 1240
6. Plan of Blair . . . Stobie 1780
7. Mrs K. Patterson

Kilmaveonaig Church rebuilt in 1591, 1794 and most recently in 1899.

four

Kilmaveonaig Church
Episcopal

Kilmaveonaig Church (Gaelic-*Cill Mo-Bheonaig*) has always traditionally been dedicated to St Adamnan, ninth abbot of Iona, who was born in 624 and died in 704. He was affectionately known as St Eonan by his followers and next to St Columba was one of the best-known and revered saints of the early Celtic church. He wrote *Life of Columba*, one of the earliest written documents about Scotland. The late Professor W J Watson, the Celtic place-names scholar, disagreed with the association with St Adamnan, arguing that the church was named after St Beoghna, second abbot of Iona, who died in 606.[1]

The church stands on the east bank of the River Tilt in the Lude estate, home from the fifteenth to the nineteenth centuries to the Robertsons of Lude, the oldest cadet branch of Clan Donnachaidh of Atholl. It was therefore closely connected with them and inside are many memorials to members of the family buried there between 1634 and 1874. Alexander Robertson of Lude died suddenly in 1639 at Dalcapon and there is a memorial stone slab to him and his mother, Agnes Gordon, on the inside north wall of the church:

> HEIR LYIS HONORABIL PERSONS AGNES
> GORDON SPOVS TO ALEX^R ROBERTSON
> OF INCHMACRANOCH DOCHTER LAVFUL
> TO THE LARD ABERGELDY DECESSIT
> 9 DECMB 1634: AND ANE VORTHE
> MAN ALEXANDER ROBERTSON THAIR
> SON LAIRD OF LUDE . . .
> MAREIT HIS TVA DOCHTERS VEIL DESSIT
> IN GREAT FAME FAVR AND VELTH 3 FEB 1639
> AND OF HIS AGE 80 YEIR

On an oak tablet on the north side of the sanctuary are recorded the following:

Alexander Robertson	died	1673	Buried here
His wife, Cath Campbell			
sister of the Earl of Breadalbane	"	1699	Finlarig
John Robertson	"	1731	here
His wife Mary Farquharson of Invercauld	"	1751	"
John Robertson	"	1741	"
and his wife the Hon. Charlotte Nairn	"	1785	"

James Robertson	died	1803	Buried here
and his wife Margaret Mercer of Aldie	"	1802	"
Col James Robertson their 2nd son	"	1820	"
General William Robertson	"	1820	"
Margaret Haldane of Gleneagles, his first wife	"	1805	"
William James Robertson, 2nd son of General Robertson	"	1813	"
Col. J A Robertson their eldest son	"	1874	"

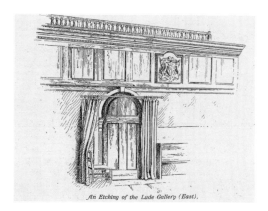

An Etching of the Lude Gallery (East).

A sketch showing the Lude Gallery (East) in Kilmaveonaig church with the door into the vault.

Beside the river there is a triangular piece of ground, now very overgrown with trees and shrubs, called Dal an t-Sagairt (*Priest's Field*), doubtless at one time part of the old church glebe. By 1794 the glebe, which occupied ground to the west of the church, was providing a rent of £10 a year.[2] It consisted of 3.38 acres of arable ground and dwelling houses and by 1815 its rent had increased to £12.[3] A little downstream was a ford called the Priest's Ford, possibly so named as it would have been used by the priest.

After the Reformation, Kilmaveonaig was rebuilt by the Robertsons in 1591 as is verified by a stone in the south wall inscribed AR AG 1591. "AR" stands for Alexander Robertson, son of John Robertson and Beatrix Gardyn, while "AG" is for his wife, Agnes Gordon. The birdcage belfry contains a bell 13⅞ inches in diameter and is inscribed: WILLIAME GLAS M. OF LITIL DINKEL 1629.[4] This bell was given to the Reverend William Glas by his wife, for her husband's church in Little Dunkeld but when he changed his allegiance, she said it would never again ring for a presbyterian service and it was sold to Kilmaveonaig. During a violent storm in 1883 a large ash tree blew down on the church, damaging the belfry and a number of tombstones. Rather than hang the bell on a nearby tree, a committee decided that the belfry should be restored and the tree sold to defray costs and it made £4.16.4 at public auction. The following lines refer to the bell:

> Oh, such a people, oh, such a people.
> Oh, such a people of Little Dunkeld;
> They have stickit their minister,
> Drowned their precentor,
> Dung doon the steeple,
> And drunken the bell.[5]

The problem of clandestine burials in Kilmaveonaig church and yard arose in 1630 when the Lude Baron Court issued the following edict:

> Nane within the parochin of Kilmavewnak burie na corpis within the Kirk thereof without leichence of the minister thereof or of the laird of Lude principal elder of the said Kirk . . . under pane of £10.[6]

Baron Courts dealt with law and order at a local level, with the local laird presiding over it himself at times. When heritable jurisdictions were largely abolished after 1747, the powers of these private courts were much diminished and they fell into disuse, being replaced by the setting up of a properly constituted system of sheriff courts.

As late as 1635 the old parish boundary was still clearly defined in rents paid "within the parish of Kilmavewnage". These were precisely outlined in a valuation of the parish by the Dunkeld Presbytery dated 29 July of that year:[7]

	£ Scots
The lands of the two Leavages [Strathgroys] and Dachin [Upper Strathgroy] pays yearly to the heretor of silver dewtie the sum of	133. 6. 8
. . . and pay by feu dewtie	32. 0. 0
and to the minister of teind silver	26. 0. 0
The lands of Balnagrew of silver dewtie yearly	166.13. 4
and to the minister for the teinds parsonage and viccarage	13. 0. 0
The lands of Balarnot and Innertilt of silver dewtie to the heretor	111.13. 4
and pays of teind silver by and allow to the minister	21.13. 4
The lands of Balnakellie of silver dewtie yearly	35.13. 4
and of teind silver to the minister for parsonage and viccarage	4. 6. 8
The lands of Pitnacrie of silver dewtie yearly	52. 0. 0
and of silver dewtie to the minister for parsonage and viccarage	8.13. 4
The lands of Kindroquhart with the miln croft by the commoditie of the miln pays yearly silver dewtie	80. 0. 0
and of the teind silver to the minister for parsonage and viccarage lands	13. 0. 0
	698. 0. 0
Add for Lude Parish containing the Monyie [Monzies] etc	208. 0. 0
	£906. 0. 0

After 1689 and the coming of the protestant William and Mary to the throne episcopacy was disestablished in Scotland so that Kilmaveonaig fell into disrepair, with only occasional maintenance undertaken by the Robertsons of Lude and Faskally and the Stewarts of Urrard. When the Reverend Walter Stewart, who lived in Orchil, died in 1728, three heritors, John Robertson of Lude, Alexander Robertson of Faskally and John Stewart of Kynachan, invited his nephew, another Walter Stewart, then minister at Doune, to fill the vacancy in Kilmaveonaig. Their first letter of 19 October was not sent, because Lude expressed doubts to his cousin, Faskally, that it contained proposals unsuitable for a minister. An example of this was . . . "and for your encouragement we promise you twenty five pounds Ster. yearly to be paid out of our hand, which is as much as you get where you are . . .". Another instance read ". . . and your countrymen hope, now that we unanimously make choice of you, that you'l frankly imbrace this, our cordial invitation home to your native country, and prevent our asking the interposition of the Bishop's authority, which we are determined to have if you refuse our kindly call." These implied threats, before the man even had a chance to reply, resulted in another draft being prepared which avoided similar improprieties.

The new draft described Walter as "the properest man and most acceptable to the generosity of those concerned in our meeting House of Atholl". The letter went on to discuss the problems "of finding any other of equal merit who knows the language and genius of the people". There was also a hint lest Walter might be "apprehensive of being molested by those disaffected to our party" and he was reassured that "our late minister lived without any disturbance of the kind". They admitted that "he had some difficulty in uplifting his small salary" but had overcome this by appointing a member of the church to collect his stipend on his behalf. The letter concluded by suggesting that " if you incline to comply with our desire which we earnestly wish, we make no doubt of the bishop's concurrence". The three heritors were eager for Walter to come to Kilmaveonaig because of his local connections and were no doubt very happy to receive his acceptance of the position on 29 October.[8]

By the middle of the eighteenth century, episcopacy was firmly re-established. In 1749 the church was surveyed and its measurements were as follows:

Length of both sides after deducting doors and pulpit	102 feet
Quire	23 feet
Wester Loft	17 feet
Easter Loft	13 feet

At this period there were two galleries in the church, the east one being above the vault where members of the Robertson of Lude family were buried.[9]

Allocation of Seats

Allocation of seating space within a church was based on the "valued rentals" of each landlord and the Duke of Atholl being the largest landowner with £2,121.13.3 Scots in rents at this time, was given the choir area, the space between that and the altar, all the south side of the church east of the east door, the north side of the altar from the door to the west gable and the whole of the west gallery. Robertson of Lude, rents £600 and Robertson of Kincraigie, rents £147.13.4, were given all the space to the south of the altar, from the choir to the west door, together with the east gallery, save for limited space for Robertson of Faskally. Stewart of Urrard, with a rental of £147.13.4 was given the area east of the pulpit, where his existing pew was located. Stewart of Bonskeid, rents £120, was allowed to retain the space previously claimed by him.[10]

No matter how carefully seating in the church was allocated, problems constantly arose. Lude, for instance, was informed of an incident that happened on 3 March 1796 when his pew was "broken in pieces and removed to another place" by the Stewart family from Balaneasie in Glen Tilt. This had been done to give them room to dig a grave where their own pew stood. At that time it was still common practice for a body to be buried inside the church, under its own pew. The report concluded : ". . . no doubt they will patch your seat together in some shape and put it in its own place again. However I think that such conduct ought not to pass unnoticed."[11]

Through the allegiance of its laird and ministers, Kilmaveonaig was closely associated with the Jacobite cause and after the defeat of Charles Edward Stuart's army at Culloden in 1746 the church was partly destroyed by government soldiers. In that same year an act of parliament was passed forbidding any episcopalian congregation to be larger than five people. Fines for contravening this were harsh but worship continued, especially in larger houses which had several rooms opening on to a hall. By having not more than five people in each room, a minister could

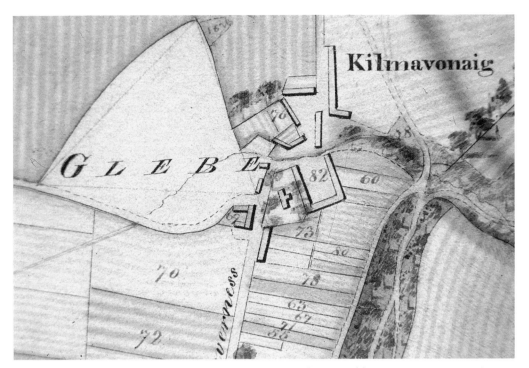

preach from the hall without technically infringing the act. These penal laws were not repealed until 1792, following the death of Charles Edward Stuart in 1788.

1794 Rebuilding

A stone in the west gable confirms that the church was rebuilt in 1794, large enough to hold 260 people. This was to a plan carried out by Charles Robertson, a mason from Cloichfoldich in Strathtay and John Stewart, wright. Sixty six persons, with a measured space of 18 inches each, sat in the east gallery, while the west gallery, which still remains, held 42 people, also with 18 inches space. The north gallery, a new addition, contained 44 seats at 17 inches each. There was room for 108 people in the well of the church at 17 inches each. This difference in "bottom size" is explained by the reason that the wider spaces were for "the quality". The altar was moved to the south side between the two windows. Pine timber from the Black Wood of Rannoch was provided for the rebuilding by Colonel Alexander Robertson of Struan, the clan chief.

At this time the minister in charge was the Reverend John Robertson, factor to the Blairfettie estate in Glen Errochty but who resided at Middleton of Derculich in Strathtay. He preached once every three weeks to a congregation which numbered about 18 families. He had two other churches in his charge, officiating also at Strathtay and Strathtummel.[12]

In 1806 it was decided to augment his stipend and £15.11.0 was raised through a collection. This was done in consideration of:

> . . . the trouble, fatigue and expences he undergoes in consequence, and that daily increasing owing to the advance upon the necessaries of life and every thing else thro' the change and alteration in the times . . . so as to enable him to continue his services.

Nearly fifty people signed and committed themselves to annual payments ranging from five pounds five shillings by General Robertson of Lude, to fifteen shillings from Mrs McDuff and Miss Stewart, Orchil; Widow Stewart, Kilmaveonaig, seven shillings and sixpence; John Moon, Aldclune, ten shillings; Alex Stewart, horse seller, Blair, five shillings; Alex Robertson, Shinagag, two shillings and sixpence and Janet Robertson, Kincraigie one shilling.[13]

At the start of the nineteenth century, Kilmaveonaig was still a thriving village, consisting of ten buildings clustered round and near the church on the main road to Inverness. There was an inn, forge and school with 120 scholars. Gradually, after the road was re-routed in the 1820s to its present line, the village fell into decay when new cottages were built at Ballentoul, now part of Bridge of Tilt, along the side of the new road, leaving only the church and graveyard to survive.

Hanging inside the church on the north and south walls there are two well-preserved hatchments of James Robertson of Lude, who died in 1803 and his wife, Margaret Mercer of Aldie. Hatchments or funeral escutcheons were hung above the main entrance of a deceased person's house for about a year, after which they were often placed in a church. Made of painted wood and canvas, they show the arms of the above husband and wife and bear the Lude motto: "Dinna wauken sleepin' dogs". Very few hatchments have survived in Scotland and they are of great interest in showing the close links that exist between heraldry and family history.[14]

The Lude estate was sold in 1821 to Mr James McInroy and ten years later the question of ownership of pews in the church rose once more. Writing to Mr William McInroy, Colonel James Robertson of Lude observed:

One of two funeral hatchments for James Robertson of Lude and his wife Margaret, which hang in Kilmaveonaig church.

17 November 1831

It is indisputable and easy to prove that with very small assistance, the whole chapel was built by my grandfather, no other family contributing more than was sufficient for the expence of a single seat, the largest of which was by Stewart of Fincastle but only the front seat. The east gallery and vault underneath was strictly for our private use and from the date of the building to the sale of the property in 1821, constantly occupied and ever since then I have retained possession of the family burial place within the chapel and do so still. How the clergyman [the Reverend John MacMillan] can pretend to acquire an authority to have the disposal of the seat is rediculous. . . .

As to the doctrines of the Scotch Episcopal Communion they have within these 6 years become so changed – they are no longer protestant having taken that name which is the glory of the British Reformation out of their prayer books canons etc. They deserve not the name even if they had retained it as they by their (so called) Bishops have

endeavoured to force into use a communion service more popish than even that of the mass itself.[15]

The Reverend John MacMillan was born in 1799 and graduated MA from Aberdeen University in 1824. His first charge was as rector of St John the Evangelist in the Black Isle until 1830 when he joined Kilmaveonaig, remaining there for four years. For the next twenty two years he was the Scottish Episcopal priest for Strathtay and was then appointed the first minister of the new St Mary's Episcopal Church in Birnam. He stayed there for the next fourteen years and died in 1870.[16]

The Reverend William Maclaurin, minister of Kilmaveonaig for six years (1834-1840) was popular with his congregation and when he was transferred to Elgin, his place was taken by the Reverend Thomas Walker (1841-1856) who lived in Middlebridge. At the time of Queen Victoria's stay in Blair Castle in 1844, her Lady in Waiting, Lady Charlotte Canning, attended a service in the church and described it thus:

> I went in the evening to the poor little Episcopal Chapel. It has bare earth between the seats and only a board to stand and kneel upon & a pathway paved. The galleries crowd it up & it might hold a number of people but only 12 were there counting the clergyman. The sermon was just after the collect & a psalm was sung by the 4 men who are usually the whole congregation. The service was very well done & I am glad to hear that poor Mr Walker is not the bad man he is represented to be.[17]

Lord Glenlyon (later the 6th Duke of Atholl) had no time for Thomas Walker, accusing him of trespassing and fishing illegally in the Tilt. During the Queen's visit, a deer drive was organised for the benefit of Prince Albert and 800 to 1,000 deer were herded and driven towards Albert's position. This immense herd was frightened off by the arrival of two men walking down the glen track, so that the prince's sport was completely ruined. One of the "intruders" was the Reverend Walker who hastily wrote his apology to Lord Glenlyon:

> 24 September 1844
>   Understanding that by my unlucky appearance in Glen Tilt last Thursday I was partly the means of turning the very fine drive of that day to the disappointment doubtless of the royal party and the consequent annoyance of your Lordship, I beg to express my deep regret that I should have been in any way the cause of the unfortunate circumstance.[18]

North view of Kilmaveonaig church before restoration in 1899.

Lord Glenlyon was furious that a day's sport, which had taken so much time and trouble to organise had been spoilt, while the prince was of the opinion that the minister should be encouraged to spend more time reading and preaching and less time "trespassing" in the forest. Thomas Walker eventually alienated most of his congregation and, declining the Bishop's offer of retirement, was locked out of his church in 1856.

The charge was vacant for the next ten years during which time it was kept going by interim parsons: 1857-1860 the Rev Stuart Robson, 1862-1864 the Rev James Robertson and the Rev J Gammack in 1865. In 1866 the Reverend Henry St John Howard was appointed minister of Holy Trinity, Pitlochry as well as Kilmaveonaig, which he described after his first visit:

> When I was appointed to the Incumbency of Pitlochrie in 1866 I found this Chapel at Kilmaveonaig in a shocking state of neglect and internal unrepair – the flooring had almost rotted away, exposing the earth; the passage was flagged with large undressed flags full of deep inequalities; there was a descent of several inches at the door from the churchyard into the chapel; the walls were mostly green with damp; between the two large windows there was a pulpit nearly as high as the gallery, and in front of it a small table covered with a moth-eaten piece of baize, which was intended for an Altar.[19]

Over the following years the Reverend Howard carried out a number of alterations and improvements:

> 1866-1869: I burnt the pulpit, placing a decent Wooden Altar . . . removed the narrow pews, refloored the Chapel, took up the flag-stones and laid down tiles; placed chairs for seats . . . 1870 took away the old stairs which were built against the outside for ascending into the gallery, and subsituted a wooden one . . . and repaired roofs. 1871 built a porch . . . and erected a stove.. repaired the Vestry within and without. 1872 Easter – The mice having eaten holes in the covering of the Altar I had given in 1866, Mrs Cunynghame (Kindrochet) presented a handsome green cloth.

In the1880s the churchyard walls being "dilapidated and ruinous", were repaired by Duncan Stewart, Fenderbridge. There was also concern about the ongoing muddy state of the church road due mainly to Stewart, the tenant farmer in Bridge of Tilt using it as a cart track and for driving his cattle. He was advised to keep the road in proper order or otherwise not use it in connection with his farm.[20]

The Reverend Christopher Bowstead, minister of Kilmaveonaig from 1891 to 1912.

Reverend Christopher Bowstead

Henry Howard died in the spring of 1891 and the Reverend Christopher Bowstead, who had taken services in 1888 and 1889, succeeded him in June of that year. He was born in Messingham, Linclonshire in 1847, son of the parish minister and a grandson of the Bishop of Lincoln. He was educated at Uppingham School, graduated from Durham University and ordained in 1872. His first appointment was in Grantham and afterwards to Croydon.[21]

Although the fabric of the church was in a reasonable state of repair, Christopher Bowstead planned a major rebuilding programme in an attempt to stem the falling numbers in the congregation. Over a period of time the east and north galleries were removed, the altar resited on the east gable and a new slate roof put on. The old earthen floor was dug up and a new wooden floor laid and seated with chairs. External harling was removed and stonework repointed. Stone mullions were put in the two south windows and wood from the old east gallery was salvaged to form a "Lude Seat" at the west end of the church for the laird and his family. The church was re-opened for worship by the bishop of the diocese on Thursday 28 July 1898, the day after the anniversary of the Battle of Killiecrankie, to a packed congregation and the event was celebrated after the service, by a gathering of clergy and friends in the Tilt Hotel.[22]

"A deplorable outrage"
Christopher Bowstead was not without his critics, especially members of the local branch of the Clan Donnachaidh Society. Mrs Sarah Robertson Matheson, the energetic honorary secretary and treasurer, convened a meeting in 1898 which was attended by the following members: James Robertson, district secretary and Alexander Robertson, corn miller, both residing in Pitlochry and joint conveners; John Robertson, Old Blair; James Robertson, Alexander Robertson and James Seaton, Pitlochry; Robert Robertson, Shierglas and the Reverend Andrew Meldrum, Logierait. A letter of apology for absence was received from Edgar Robertson, laird of Auchleeks, who expressed his sympathy with the purpose of the meeting and his readiness "to remedy a deplorable outrage".[23]

Stone tablet above Kilmaveonaig church door with the date of the third restoration.

The so-called outrage related to the time during rebuilding of the church when the earth floor, particularly that part under the old east gallery was dug up and the committee expressed their disapproval:

> The committee entertain no doubt whatever that the large quantity of soil now lying in an extended heap against the churchyard back wall, now containing many fragments of human bones, was excavated from the burying ground of the Robertson lairds of Lude.[24]

Several options were discussed about the best method of disposing of the soil. Firstly "that the soil be placed within the church walls in its former situ" but this was rejected because of the difficulty of doing so owing to the advanced state of the repairs and "to obviate friction and unpleasant jarrings that would inevitably emerge". The second option was "that a large pit be formed in an unoccupied part of the churchyard". This was passed unanimously as was the decision that "the cartful that had been taken to the Episcopal clergyman's garden at Invertilt" should also be returned. The pit was to be dug at the back of the church with a retaining wall 4½ to 5½ feet high. Between this wall and the ground rising and sloping to the back wall of the churchyard, there would be a cavity large enough to take all the soil excavated from the floor of the church.

Bowstead agreed to this and also to replace all the tombstones, coats of arms, memorial tablets and hatchments which had been removed to the area of the former Lude vault, in the chancel. The local clan society committee concluded by expressing:

> . . . their strongest disapproval of the actions of the Episcopal clergyman at Pitlochry and those associated with him for wanton interference with an

ecclesiastical fabric, and with the dust of the departed reposing within its walls, without either the permission or the sanction of the properly and legally constituted authorities.[25]

The matter even came to the notice of the press at this time, an example being this somewhat tongue-in-cheek letter to the *People's Journal* :

THE DESECRATION AT KILMAVEONAIG CHURCH, BLAIR-ATHOLL
Sir – In connection with the sacrilegious digging up and carting away of human bones at above church, can any of your readers tell me where the following old rhyme is to be found?

When Kilmaveonaig's dead shall lie
Long weeks exposed beneath the sky,
Woe to the priest the wreck that planned!
Woe to the race that holds Lude land!
Glad am I, though my bones be there,
I shall not live to shed a tear.
I am etc
"DINNA WAUKEN SLEEPING DOGS."

John Robertson in Old Blair, factor to the Duke of Atholl, wrote to the laird of Lude to commiserate: ". . . no one regrets more than I do the publicity that has been given to this matter. . . . I have been disgusted with a notice which appeared in the People's Journal." He had attended the meeting solely because the Reverend Andrew Meldrum was to be there, knowing that he was a "sensible man who would see what was being done with the earth". Bowstead, although denying the extent of the removal of earth and bones, appeared somewhat chastened and admitted that the Lude Robertson motto was "sage advice".[26]

In 1906, Christopher Bowstead built a house in Bridge of Tilt called Dail an t-Sagairt. He included an oratory on the south side beside the front door. This contained a paten and chalice belonging to the church and a memorial cross to the Reverend Henry Howard. Bowstead "lavished all his care and devoted affection for nearly twenty years" on the restoration of Kilmaveonaig Church and when he died on 19 August 1925, the north window was dedicated to his memory.

He was succeeded by the Reverend Edward Cooke 1912-1918, then B R Blakiston 1919; Herbert McNaught 1920-1938; Leopold Critchley 1939-1950; Farquhar Macintyre 1950-1956; Derrick Burke 1957-1963; Duncan Maclean 1963-1970; Ambrose Barcroft 1970-1982; Colin Preston-Thomas 1982-1993; Michael Henly 1993-1995, when Roger Devonshire took over.

The Baptist Church

More than thirty years before the Disruption of 1843, "missionaries" were moving through the Highlands of Scotland, preaching a robust, evangelical message, which sent out shock-waves through the established and other churches. They founded a number of Baptist churches, one of which was a thatched building, put up in 1821 in the village of Kilmaveonaig, at a cost of £34.16.8. It was large enough to hold 200 people and was under the charge of William Tulloch, who was born in the parish of Abernethy in 1776. He converted to the Baptist faith in 1808, was stationed at Lawers before becoming a pastor in Aberfeldy and then Blair Atholl in 1819. He developed "the home circuit" which he covered in winter and in 1821 was described as follows:

> The districts in which I labour, when at home at Kilmaveonaig, are Atholl and its neighbouring glens, Rannoch, Foss, Strath Tummel, Glenfonchastel, Moulin, Sless Beag and sometimes by way of Glen-Briarchan. . . .

In the summer his circuits were much larger and lasted up to nine weeks and included Strathspey, Fort William, Lismore, Mull, Iona, Oban and Lorn.[27]

In an 1820 review of churches in the area, the Rev. John Stewart, the Blair Atholl parish minister, complained that:

> Such indeed is the laudable attitude of the people to public worship that where they have not an opportunity of a facility in the established church, they will attend without having any regard for the man or his particular doctrine, the meetings of a wandering baptist preacher who lives at Kilmaveonaig – and to complete the list of defectors it may be necessary to state that of his persuasions there are 5 heads of families in the whole parish.[28]

A new baptist church was built at Ballentoul in Bridge of Tilt in 1836, when 60 communicants, 31 from Blair Atholl and 29 from adjacent parishes formed its congregation. Complete immersion of the person to be baptised did not take place in the church but in a selected spot in the River Tilt, provided the supplicant was fit enough! This church closed in 1886 and was subsequently converted to a private house.

Two second-generation Gaelic-speaking preachers, John McLellan, born in Glenlyon and William Tulloch, Junior, born in Blair Atholl in 1822, became

The former baptist church in Ballentoul, now a private house.

prominent leaders of the Baptist movement in Scotland. John McLellan was the Blair Atholl missionary from 1860-1868, before moving to Cupar and Duncan Street churches, Edinburgh, as pastor. In 1883 he was appointed Baptist Union tutor in Systematic Theology, before the establishment of a baptist college. William Tulloch served in Elgin, Edinburgh and Dundee, before becoming secretary of the Baptist Union of Scotland in 1869 and then its president in 1882.[29]

References

1. *History of the Celtic Place-names of Scotland,* Watson
2. BCCR Bundle 1228
3. BCCR Trunk 9 V 6
4. PSAS Volume 122
5. *Facts and Fancies about Kilmaveonaig,* Bowstead
6. SRO GD 50/159
7. Holy Trinity Church Records
8. Ibid
9. SRO GD 132/730/1
10. Ibid
11. SRO GD 132/731
12. *Facts and Fancies about Kilmaveonaig,* Bowstead
13. Holy Trinity Church Records
14. CDA 1960
15. SRO 132/797/1
16. *A Quest for an Ancestor,* Smith
17. *Charlotte Canning,* Surtees
18 *Queen Victoria's Scottish Diaries,* Kerr
19. *Facts and Fancies about Kilmaveonaig,* Bowstead
20. Ibid
21. Kilmaveonaig Records
22. *Facts and Fancies about Kilmaveonaig,* Bowstead
23. Holy Trinity Records
24. Ibid
25. Ibid
26. Ibid
27. TGSI Volume LVI
28. BCCR Bundle 1228
29. TGSI Volume LVI

five

Struan Church
Glen Errochty

Struan (Gaelic-*Sruthan*) means Place of Streams reflecting its situation at the confluence of two rivers, the Garry and the Errochty. *Errochty* means an assembly or meeting place, which in the past was often at a confluence, so this is an indication of the importance of Struan from early times.[1] The area of land at the meeting point of these two rivers was known as Socach Struan, *Socach* being the Gaelic for a ploughshare, which exactly describes the shape of the ground there.

In former times the church was known as the church of St Fillan and the outline of the footings of an older building can still be seen in the churchyard. At one time it contained a statue of its patron saint, whose feet in times of drought were dipped in the nearby St Fillan's Well, at the foot of Tom an Tigh Mhor. This

Undated plan of Struan showing the settlement and churchyard with the former church sited in the middle rather than to the north side as now.

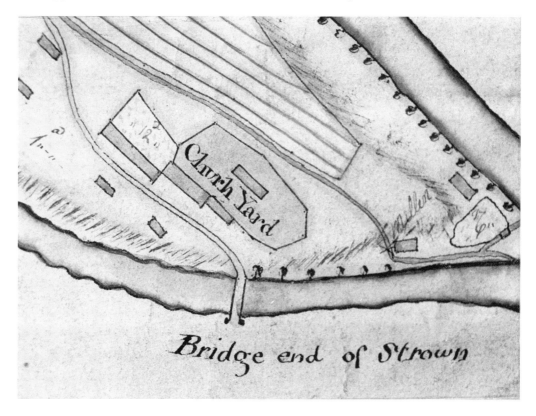

is an artifical motte or mound upstream from the church, on the south bank of the Garry and reckoned to be an early stronghold of the chiefs of Clan Donnachaidh. The statue somehow survived beyond the Reformation, until one minister, the Reverend John Hamilton, outraged by this continuation of a popish practice, smashed the statue and flung the broken pieces into the Garry below. It seems the minister paid dearly for this deed, for soon afterwards his son died, quite insane. There is an ironic twist to this tale, as one of the attributes of the water from the well was a cure for insanity.[2]

John Hamilton was put forward as the minister for Blair Atholl in July 1717 and ordained on 25 February 1718.[3] The duchess wrote of her "hearty concurrence with the presbytery in their choice, the people having signified their willingness to have him settle amongst them as their minister." He became moderator of the Dunkeld Presbytery in 1720 and was transferred to Kenmore parish in 1723.[4]

The glebe of Struan was feued in 1732 to James Robertson of Kindrochet, a vassal of the Robertsons of Faskally, for one merk (13/4 Scots).[5] This contract was with the Duke of Atholl, who had previously acquired the land, as is indicated in a note on the agreement: "His Grace acquired the right to this Gleib by an exchange with the minister of Blair".[6]

St Fillan's market was held on the saint's day, the first Friday in the new year (old style), about 20 January (new style), in a field immediately to the west of the church, called Croft an Taggart (*Priest's Croft*) and it continued on long after the Reformation.[7]

Feu of Struan glebe in 1732.

St Fillan's Bell

The iron bell of St Fillan, measuring 10½ inches in height and 7 inches wide, was housed in the church and is a typical example of bells of the early Celtic Church period. It remained in use until the nineteenth century when William McInroy of Lude presented the church with a new black, 14-inch diameter bell, with no visible inscription. It hangs in the stone belfry which was renewed in 1996. St Fillan's bell is now housed in Perth Museum and nineteen of these ancient bells are known to have survived from the time of the early Scottish church.[8]

A story about St Fillan's bell relates that it was stolen by a man from Rannoch, who wished to transfer the reputed protection and privileges of the patron saint to his own district. Pausing in his flight home to rest a little, at the top of Bohespic hill, he placed the bell on a rock. When the time came to move on, the bell proved immovable – it was seemingly stuck fast to the stone. Seeing this as a sign of the saint's displeasure, he immediately became alarmed and at once resolved to return the bell. As soon as he faced back in the direction of Struan, the bell freed itself and was restored to its rightful place by its "penitent bearer".[9]

For centuries Struan and its church has been associated with Clan Donnachaidh or the Robertsons of Atholl. Many chiefs were buried beneath the old church floor and evidence of this is recorded in the *Chronicle of Fortingall* from the *Black Book of Taymouth:*

> Obiit Alexander M'James alias Robertson . . . prope Strowen in Autholia et tumultatus in ecclesia de Strowan xix[mo] die Januarii anno Domini M V[c] lv.

and

> Obiit Robertus Robertson de Strowen apud Innervack vi[ce]simo tertio die Mai anno Domini M V[c] sexte sex yeris et tumultatus in ecclesia de Strowen die supra dicto. . . .

Perhaps the most noteworthy of the chiefs to be buried there was Alexander Robertson, the great Jacobite suppporter born around 1670. Popularly known as the "Poet Chief" he had a flair for acid wit and acute observation. The *Scots Magazine* recorded his death on 18 April 1749:

> At his house at Carie, in Rannoch, Perthshire, in the 81st year of his age, a bachelor, Alexander Robertson of Struan, chief of his clan.

He did not go to his grave unmourned as two thousand people of all ranks followed the coffin the eighteen miles from Carie to its final resting place at Struan.

In more recent times the Clan Donnachaidh Society has donated items in memory of clansfolk who have worshipped there over the centuries. The principal gift is an oak font with a dove motif carved on one side and containing a silver bowl, to symbolise the descent of the Holy Spirit at baptism. The second memorial is a carved and coloured panel of the four evangelists, while a carved wooden panel bearing a gilded and coloured clan crest at the top records the gifts and their dedication in the church:

CHUM GLOIR DHÉ
The Clan Donnachaidh Society
Beautified this Church of their Fathers
as a Memorial to Generations of Clansmen
who worshipped in this House of God. 1960.

Struan Elders
The Kirk Session minutes for 11 September 1718 records "a List of the most judicious honest and knowing men in the west end of the paroch to be elders . . ." who were:

> Alexander Robertson and John Robertson alias McInduine, both in Bohespick; John Calmanich in Grenich; Alexander Steuart in Balnabodich, both in Strathtumble.
> In Glenerochty – John Steuart, Tulloch; Patrick Robertson, Blairphety; John McLean, Trinafure;
> Charles Robertson, Kinaldy;
> Donald Robertson, Wester Blairphettie;
> Mr James Robertson in Auchlix.
> From Glengarry, they were Duncan Robertson, Daltaranny;
> John Duff, Dalnamoon;
> Donald Robertson, Dalinreich;
> James Robertson, Clunes;
> John Cameron, Calavine; Aeneas Robertson, Pitagowan;
> Donald McPharland, Calabruar;
> Alexander Forbes, Pitaldonich.[10]

At a kirk session meeting held in Struan on 9 May 1742, specific districts were allotted thus, following the old Struan parish:

> Their several Quarters were assigned to each Elder as follows –
> To James Robertson in Craig, from Callavin to Dallnakeardich, [and] to Pittagoun from Callavin to the Duke of Atholl's Parks in the north of Garrie and the two Invervacks and Kindrochitts ground, on the south side of the Garrie;
> To Alexander Robertson in Kinaldie, from Kindrochitts march to the head of Glen Errichity on both sides of the water;
> To James Robertson Tombicaldonich, from Dalnakeardich to Auchleanie, the town itself included;
> To Donald McColman in Grennich, from the Burn of Tressaid to Strowan's march with Bohespick;
> To Thomas McColman in Balnambodich from the said Burn of Tressaid to ffincastles march, Borannich of Bonskeid included.[11]

1727 Repairs
By the 1720s both the Blair Atholl and Struan churches, as well as the Blair Atholl manse were in need of repair. A meeting in December 1727 between the Dunkeld Presbytery and local heritors appointed Adam Brown, mason, Patrick McInness and John Lauder, wrights and John McCraw and Andrew McMillan, slaters, who were:

> . . . solemnly sworn to bring a true and faithful verdict what it will take to repair the Kirks of Blair and Struan and also to repair the manse of Blair and what it will take to put a roof on the stipell.[12]

John Stewart, Charles Conacher and George Ritchie, birliemen in the parish, were also solemnly sworn to:

> . . . Inspect the churches of Blair Atholl and Struan and the manse and offices and bring in an estimate and verdict what it will take to repair the same for materials, workmanship and carriage.

By noon the next day Adam Brown was ready to give his costs for mason work at Struan.[13]

		£ Scots
Item:	40 bolls of lime for harling and building	26.13. 4
Item:	Taking down a rood and 3 ells	3. 0. 0
Item:	For building said work	19.10. 0
Item:	For winning stone for building kirkyard dyke and three days harling	46. 0. 0
Mason work		£95. 3. 4

Slater's costs were as follows:[14]

		£ Scots
Item:	300 Skeillie	3. 0. 0
Item:	500 nails	1.10. 0
Item:	Boll of lime for a window skew and 4 foot of rigan stone	1.19. 4
Item:	Workmanship	15. 9. 0
Slater work		£21.18. 4

The costs of repairing Struan church and its churchyard amounted to £117.1.8 Scots, equivalent to about £10 Sterling. Apart from the roof and repairs to the churchyard, only minor repairs were deemed necessary.

1742 Repairs
Within fifteen years however, major repairs were required for the two churches and the manse. John Sanders and James Robertson, masons from Dunkeld, submitted their estimate for Struan on 25 November 1742:[15]

		£ Scots
Item:	Taking down and rebuilding 3 roods and 2 ells of mason work at £15 per rood	48.16. 0
Item:	Stopping 2 windows and 22 feet Skews, winning and dressing	9.12. 0
Item:	For quarry stones needed	8. 0. 0
Item:	90 bolls of lime for building work and pinning and harling said church, inside and out	72. 0. 0
Item:	Lime for said pinning and harling, 24 bolls	14. 8. 0
Mason work		£152.16. 0
Item:	Carriage of 116 bolls of lime at 6d (Ster.) per boll	34.16. 0
Item:	Carriage of stones and sand	27. 8. 0
	Cost of carriage	£62. 4. 0

The estimate for wright work by James Gentle and John Lauder was as follows:[16]

		£ Scots
Item:	12 trees at 18 foot long 6 inches broad for 6 cuples and 6 trees for scaffolding at 20d per piece	18. 0. 0
Item:	120 dales at 8d (Ster.) per dale	48. 0. 0
Item:	7,500 double plenshions	19.12. 0
Item:	300 double floorings	1.16. 0
Item:	2 doors, 2 door frames 3 trees and 14 dales and 5 window shutters, 8 dales	11.16. 0
Item:	Mounting scaffold and taking down the old roof	15. 0. 0
Item:	Binding 6 cuples, mending, setting up and sarking the roof	33. 0. 0
Item:	Making 2 double door cases and 5 windows 2 foot wide and 4 foot high	17.10. 0
Item:	2 locks and 1 pair of crooks and bands to 5 shutters and making 5 pairs of bands	8.16. 0
Item:	Making a new pulpit with a seat for the precentor and workmanship	44. 0. 0
Wright work		£217.10. 0
Item:	Carriage of trees and dales	£ 20. 0. 0

The estimate submitted by Thomas Clark, slater from Dunkeld was as follows:[17]

		£ Scots
Item:	4 roods and 15 ells at £18 per rood	79.10. 0
Item:	4 roods and 15 ells at £10 per rood	44.15. 0
Item:	18,00 nails	42. 0. 0
Item:	24 foot of rigan stones and taking down the old slates	16.16. 0
Slater work		£183. 1. 0
Item:	Carriage of slates 210 horse and 6 horse for rigan stones and nails £9	£219. 0. 0

The estimate for the glazing by Duncan Forbes from Tulliemet was as follows:

		£ Scots
Item:	For workmanship	7.17. 0
	Carriage	2. 6
		£7.19. 6

These estimates provide a great deal of information about the former Struan church in the 1740s. The wright work tells us there were two sets of double doors, together with five shuttered windows measuring two feet wide and four feet high, each with locks and bands. A new pulpit with precentor's desk was built and much of the roof was renewed.

Dividing the Cost
In April 1743 the presbytery met with the kirk session and parish minister Alexander Stewart, to discuss the cost of renovations carried out on the two churches and manse and to divide this up amongst the heritors. The total cost of materials and labour amounted to £1,742.4.4 Scots and for carriage, £787.12.3

Scots. Each heritor's share depended on his "valued rents" received and these totals were therefore split up accordingly: [18]

Heritor	Rent £ Scots	Materials/ Workmanship Costs £ Scots	Carriage £ Scots
James Robertson, Lude	600. 0. 0	269. 5.11	115. 4. 1
Alexander Robertson, Struan	270. 0. 0	121. 3. 8	51.16. 7
George Robertson, Faskally	303.13. 0	36.17. 6	58.11. 2
Duncan Robertson, Auchleeks	80. 0. 0	35.18. 2	15. 7. 2
Patrick McGlashan, Lamton	20. 0. 0	8.19. 6	3.11.11
James Robertson, Blairfettie	120. 0. 0	53.17. 2	22.17.10
John Stewart, Bonskeid	120. 0. 0	53.17. 2	22.17.10
Patrick Robertson, Trinafour	64. 8. 9	29. 2. 4	12. 9. 7
Charles Stewart, Bohalie, for Portnelan	21. 4.10	9. 8. 6	4. 0. 7
David Robertson, Kincraigie	147.13. 4	65.19. 6	28. 4. 6
James Robertson, Kindrochet	35. 0. 0	15.14. 2	6.14. 4
Donald Robertson, Pitagowan	45. 0. 0	20. 3.11	8.12. 9
John Stewart, Fincastle, for Carrick	7. 0. 0	3. 1. 8	1. 6.10
John Stewart for Tenandry	1 47.13. 5	66. 8. 6	28. 8. 4
Duke of Atholl	2,121.13. 3	952. 8 . 4	407. 8 . 9
	£4,103.6. 7	£1,742. 4. 4	£787.12. 3

The heritors were asked to pay their proportions to Robert Stewart from Cluny, whom they had selected as their factor for this purpose.

Kirk Session

Kirk sessions were formed soon after the Reformation and were chosen from the congregation in every parish, very much as at present. It consisted of the minister and a number of men picked for their good influence and social position. They were responsible for the good conduct and morality of a parish, including discipline. The most common form of punishment for a wrongdoer was public appearance in church on the "stool of repentance" in an open space in front of the pulpit. The subject of censure was placed on this to receive their public rebuke.

Breaking of observance of the Lord's Day was a serious offence and care and attention was devoted to finding out the truth, as in this case, when a special session meeting was held in Strathtummel about an alleged affray:

Grennich 19 November 1744
    Session called . . . to examine into the ryot said to be committed by John McDonald and Elspeth McGlashan in Grennich upon Sunday the 14th October last which day Elspeth Mackglashan confessed that she threw a stone at the sd. John McDonald, which stone missed him and John in a passion did beat the said Elspeth with a tree or staff very cruelly.

The session found that Elspeth, although she did not hit John, had provoked him and was the aggressor. She was found guilty of a breach of the Sabbath and was fined £2 Scots (3/4d Sterling). John was found guilty of a "great ryot in a notorious breach of Sabbath" and fined £8 Scots (13/4d Sterling). John appeared for public rebuke in Struan church on 21 April 1745 when his fine was reduced to 2 shillings Sterling. [19]

In 1754 the gallery of the old church was in need of repair:

Blair August 11th 1754
. . . Then he [minister] proposed to make up the loft of Strowan, and to set all the pews upon the parishioners for so much yearly; to be paid to the poor. And the money designed for Glen Tilt bridge would be employed for said use in part of the charges to which the session consented. . . .[20]

December 8th 1754
. . . Alex Stewart, wright in Blairuachdar got a Portuguese piece of 36 shillings sterling of which he lent himself 7sh 6d ster. more, giving him 3sh 10d ster for his workmanship & buying materials for the loft of Strowan. . . .[21]

December 15th 1754
. . . Alex Stewart, wright in Blairuachdar got nine shillings ster. of his workmanship for the loft of Strowan, so that the session is yet due him £1.0.1⅔d ster. The smith got three shillings for his workmanship. . . .[22]

In less than three years there was trouble over misuse of the gallery and damage caused to it:

Strowan, July 29th 1757
William Mackenzie, miller at Strowan who with several others were making use of the loft of the church of Strowan and with that leaving the door open, was broken up by the wind which brought charges upon the Session to the smith for mending the bands and nails and to said Donald McFarlane for timber in mending said door. . . .[23]

Strowan Sept. 4th 1757
Wm Mckenzie and John Forbes in Kirktown of Strowan paid sixpence each and Tullich paid two pence and Patrick McLaren there is to pay a sixpence ster. for making use of the loft indecently by putting their lint in it, so that as minuted, the doors and bands of said loft were broken. . . .[24]

Blair Dec 20th 1761
. . . and this day's collection amounting in both to £1.18.1 Scots which was given to William Young wright at Invervack for mending the two doors of the church of Strowan and furnishing timber and nails thereto. . . .[25]

St Fillans appears to have been a dark, ill-lit church as the minutes of the heritors' meeting on 8 December 1791 would indicate:

. . . whereas the pulpit in the church is badly lighted the meeting recommends to Mr Mclagan [the minister] to cause a sky light of 4 panes of glass to be made where he thinks most proper. . . .[26]

Blair 9th March 1793
. . . session expended 15sh ster. for a sky light above the Pulpit of Strowan. . . .[27]

Around 1790 the churchyard dyke was rebuilt by Colonel Alexander Robertson of Struan, who also paid for the gallery built around 1800, which, according to presbytery "he lets to the best advantage".[28]

Church Affray
Details of an affray in the church were reported to the Atholl factor in September 1797. Donald MacMillan from Calvine complained that Peter Robertson from Dalnacardoch was "spreading falsehoods about him". The trouble had arisen five or six years earlier when a number of Tenandry tenants, whose land had been bought from Faskally by the Duke of Atholl, were occupying seats in the church. Donald had managed to secure a pew, which he held until 1797 when Peter Robertson:

> . . . came and possessed himself in a masterful manner before I went to the church and when I offered to sit in my own seat, Robertson rose with a stick in his hand and was to strick or nock me down till another man took hold of his stick since he would not get liberty to nock me down, He throwed me among two or three other seats till I was greatly injured in my person. When I got up I told him the seat was mine which he refused. Please I want nothing but justice which I hope you'll let me have.[29]

Gaelic services took place in Struan on every third Sunday while worship was conducted in English and Gaelic in St Brides on two successive Sundays. An 1818 report cast doubt whether communion had ever been held in St Fillans:

> The Sacrament of the Lord's Supper has been from time immemorial dispensed at the church of Blair Atholl and there only. There are something like communion tables at Blair – there are none at Struan.[30]

In that same year, the parish minister, the Reverend John Stewart, with the support of the 4th Duke of Atholl, proposed that Struan church should be "suppressed" and a new church, capable of holding the entire parish under one roof be built "at the gate of Blair Castle". Details of this proposal, which was abandoned, appear in chapter seven.

Church in Decay
According to a letter written to Frederick Graham, the Atholl factor, by James Robertson of Kindrochet, Struan church was in a ruinous state in the early 1800s:

> 31 October 1825
> . . . the present old church at Strowan is in so ruinous a state that it is really disgraceful to see it used as a place of worship for so numerous a congregation. The general opinion of the heretors seems to be that a neat, but very plain building of a sufficient size to accommodate a number equal to the present congregation, in general about 500 would suffice at Strowan.
> The expence of such a building cannot be great, besides the inhabitants of the west end of the parish are so anxious to have the church of Strowan rebuilt, that I know they will cheerfully perform the carriage of all the slates and also the greater part of the timber that may be required, which would be a considerable saving.[31]

Robert Robertson of Auchleeks maintained that St Fillans church should be rebuilt, writing: "That the church needs rebuilding no one disputes. Its present state is a disgrace to a Christian community." At the same time, the fabric of the church was surveyed by masons who reported: "The walls and roof of said church are in a quite ruinous state, incapable of repair. The length is 72 feet and breadth 17 feet. The height of the walls is 9 feet."[32]

Before a new church could be built, an extensive questionnaire was submitted by the Commission "for Plantations of Kirks . . . to build new churches". This had to be completed by the minister and elders and the questions and answers are reproduced in full.

HIGHLAND CHURCHES

Questions for building additional places of worship in the Highlands and Islands of Scotland.

1.Q   What is the length of the Parish?

A   Extreme length of the Parish is 22 miles and inhabited portion about 14 miles.

2.Q   What is its breadth?

A   Breadth of inhabited parts of Parish varies from 3 to 10 miles.

3.Q   What is the population?

A   Population according to official returns 1821 – 2455 persons.

4.Q   In what degree is the face of the country mountainous and what is the state of the roads?

A   The country is mountainous. The roads along the vallies are good but the roads or paths across the hills which divide the vallies are very bad.

5.Q   Are there any villages in the Parish and what is the amount of the respective Population of each?

A   There are no villages of consequence in the Parish and the Population of the largest Hamlet does not exceed 100.

6.Q   What is the size of the present church, and how is it situated, with respect to the villages to the centre, and to the extremes of the Parish?

A   A new church is at present in progress of building, calculated to accommodate about 600 persons within half a mile of the old church at Blair Atholl which has been condemned and in a situation more convenient for the Parishioners than that church; the new church is situated within 3 miles of the east end of the Parish, and in a populous part of it.

7.Q   Is access to the church rendered difficult by the intervention of rivers, lakes or arms of the sea? And if the Parish consists of Islands or if there be any islands in it, what is their distance from each other, and what is their respective population?

A   Access to the church of Blair Atholl is frequently rendered difficult (particularly in the winter months) for a great proportion of the Parishioners who live on the south side of the river Garry, by the intervention of that rapid stream. There are two ferries on the Garry, the one within a quarter of a mile and the other within two miles of the Church of Blair Athole, but neither of these ferries are passable when the River is in flood, and the nearest bridge upon it is five miles distant from the Church of Blair. There are no islands in the Parish.

8.Q   In what county is the Parish Church situated and within the bounds of what Presbytery?

A   The Parish is situated in the County of Perth and within the bounds of the Presbytery of Dunkeld.

9.Q   Who is the minister incumbent?

A   The Reverend John Stewart.

10.Q   Is there a second church or chapel in the Parish? And if there is, how often does the clergyman perform divine service in it?

A   There is a second church in the Parish in which divine service is performed by a Parish minister once in three weeks. This church is in a most ruinous condition and it is upon its site that is proposed to erect the church now applied for, for reasons to be specified in Answers 14 and 15.

11.Q   Are there any missions on the Royal Bounty in the Parish? And if so what are the established stations and how often is worship performed at these stations?

A   There are no missions on the Royal Bounty in the Parish.

12.Q   Are there any places of worship in the Parish not connected with the established church, how are they situated, of what description and what proportion of the Population belongs to them?

A   There is one Episcopal Chapel in the Parish, situated within a quarter of a mile of the new church building near Blair Atholl. The proportion of the population belonging to this Chapel is very inconsiderable, not more than 30 to 40 adults.

13.Q   How near are the churches of the adjoining Parishes to the confines of the Parish and have these churches any accommodation for strangers?

A   No other parish church is within such a distance of any part of this parish as would enable the parishioners to avail themselves of any accommodation it might afford. The church of Muline which is the nearest to the eastward is six miles from the extreme east end of the Parish. The Church of Kingussie in Inverness-shire, the nearest in a north-west direction, is 20 miles from any inhabited part of this parish and the Parish Churches of Dull and Fortingall are 12 miles distant in a southwest direction.

14.Q   Where is it desired that the new Church should be built and what number of persons to accommodate?

A   It is desired to have the new church built at Strowan on the site of the present ruinous church, as stated in Answer 10, about five miles west of the new church of Blair Athole, on a point of land at the junction of the Rivers Garry and Erochy, with a Bridge upon each of these rivers near to it. The number of persons it is proposed to accommodate is six hundred.

15.Q   To what part of the Parish and to what proportion of the population will the proposed new church be more convenient in respect of distance or other obstructions than the present church?

A   The proposed new establishment will be more convenient in respect of distance and other obstructions than the church of Blair Athole to the whole of the west end of the Parish consisting of the following districts or divisions, viz: Borrenich, Strathtumble, Bohespick, Glenerochy, Glen Garry, and that portion of the ancient Parish of Strowan in the immediate vicinity of the church and within two miles of it, on both banks of the River Garry. The population of these districts or divisions is about one thousand five hundred and fifty. Strowan is the most central as well as the most convenient situation that can be selected for the numerous inhabitants of the districts or portions of the united Parishes for whose benefit the new additional church is required. It has moreover the advantage (a considerable one in the estimation of the people) of there having been a place of worship there and also a place of sepulture for a great portion of the Parishioners from time immemorial.

16.Q Would the additional church from its situation be a convenient place of worship for the extremes of any of the adjoining parishes?

A The new establishment would be a convenient Place of Worship for the inhabitants of Fincastle & Bohally, portions of the Parish of Dull.

17.Q Are the heritors willing to give gratuitously the ground necessary for the site of the Church and Manse and for the the churchyard and garden? Or if not, what is the price expected?

A The ground for the site of the church and the churchyard will be given gratuitously (and for the manse and garden to the extent of an acre and a half if necessary)

18.Q Would the heritors be inclined to give the additional accommodation of a few acres of ground to the minister to enable him to keep a horse and cow?

A Heritors are willing to give four or five acres at a little distance from the manse and garden for this purpose if required.

19.Q Is there any building already erected in the Parish which might with advantage be fitted up as an additional Church? Would such a building be given gratuitously for that purpose? Or if not, what is the price demanded for it?

A There is no building at present in the Parish that could with advantage be fitted as a place of Worship.

20.Q Is there any, and what manufacture or fishery carried on in the parish?

A There is no manufacture or fishery carried on in the Parish, it being quite inland. The inhabitants follow pastoral or agricultural pursuits.

21.Q Is there any other, and what, matter connected with the object of this application?[33]

As plans for building a new church progressed, there were doubts, particularly from some Robertson heritors, that this would actually happen, as one of them, Robert Robertson of Auchleeks wrote to the Duke of Atholl:

1 June 1825
. . . from an apprehension of mischief from our minister here, who has always been allowed to interfere too much in this matter. By his officious interference with the Dunkeld Presbytery he may procure an affirmative answer to this question and thereby defeat our object of procuring a new church. It is impossible to say what may be the real motive of the Minister whether he conceive it likely to accelerate or retard his quitting the manse. He appears to be decidedly hostile to the measure.[34]

Presbytery Approval
On 29 March 1825 the Dunkeld Presbytery approved the building of a new church at Struan as the minutes record:

As to the proposed erection at Struan in the parish of Blair Atholl and Struan, the Presbytery are of opinion, that an erection at Struan or somewhere in that neighbourhood is highly expedient.[35]

*Struan church,
built in 1828,
above the bridge
over the River
Errochty.*

A plan to site the new church behind the ruinous one was drawn up and submitted to the heritors of the parish by James Robertson of Kindrochet in October 1827. The new building was to be capable of holding 500 people, allowing 18 inches for each sitter but this number was considered too large, and 400 was regarded as a more reasonable estimate.[36] John Stewart from Woodend was therefore commissioned to check on the size of the congregation and he reported that on 4 November there were 351 people present.[37] Three weeks later the number had dropped to 245.[38] It was therefore agreed that the seating be reduced to 450 and a small comfortable vestry added. The minister insisted on this, stating it "to be indispensable – having hitherto been obliged to pay rent for a very uncomfortable place for the purpose".[39]

Written estimates were received from the following builders:[40]

David Nelson	£470.0.0
Charles Sim	£455.0.0
Alexander Sim	£450.0.0

Alexander Robertson and John Angus, builders in Dunkeld studied the plan, but being unable to visit the site, were unsure where to obtain building materials and could not give a proper estimate. They guessed the cost would be in the region of £720.[41] Alexander Sim tendered the cheapest quote but indicated that he needed eighteen months to complete the job. This was deemed an unacceptable length of time for the parish to wait for a new church.

Charles Sim, from Edradynate in Strathtay, described as a "good tradesman who had built the Blair Manse and offices", was awarded the contract, although the duke had stipulated that costs should not exceed £450. The heritors confirmed the award of the contract to Charles Sim:

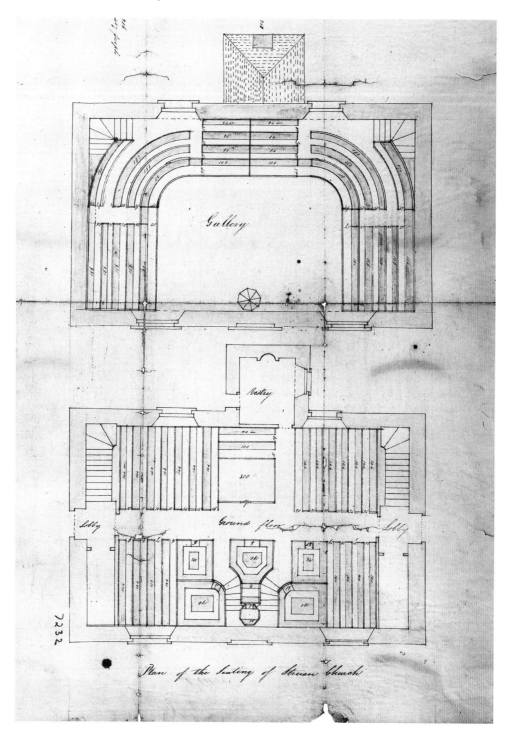

An 1830 seating plan for the ground floor and gallery of Struan church.
(Scottish Record Office RHP 7232)

10 January 1828

For ourselves and the other heritors of the united parishes of Blair Atholl and Strowan we hereby accept your offer for building a church at Strowan for the sum of 4 hundred and fifty five Pounds Sterling agreeable to the plan and specifications prepared by you. . . .[42]

The interior of Struan church, where "there is a sense of peace and stillness that speaks to the hearing ear."

Charles Christie, the duke's carpenter, was asked to check over the building at the beginning of November, before the heritors inspected it and he found "the whole work well executed and according to the specification." A meeting duly took place on 13th November at which it was agreed that the pulpit canopy with the book board should be corrected and that some of the doors, particularly on the precentor's desk and in the gallery were stiff.[43] The churchyard dyke on the north side had been taken down to make way for the new building and Sim agreed to repair this for £14, "having his people and materials still on the spot". All considered the church "well finished" and the key was handed over to the minister who preached his first sermon in the new church on 16 November 1828.[44]

Seat Allocation

A memorandum "of the number of seats and measurements of each seat in the Division of the church of Strowan among the Heritors" was drawn up on 25 October 1831. This covered the 57 pews in the church – 31 on the ground floor and 26 in the gallery. The pulpit was designated Number 1. Number 2 was the clerk's desk and 3 was set aside for the elders. Number 4 was for the Duke of Atholl's trustees and the major share, pews 5-30 were allocated to the Atholl estate tenants. Number 31 was for the minister's family.

Up in the gallery, 32-34 were for Auchleeks, 35, 36 and 41 were again for the Atholl trustees and 37-39 and 48 were again for Atholl tenants. Blairfettie was given pew 40. Tenandry was allocated 42-44, Dr Stewart of Bonskeid 45

The 4-foot high pillar stone in Struan churchyard.

The Pictish Stone housed in Struan church shows a double disc bisected by a Z-shaped rod.

and 46, while 47 was for Fincastle, 49 to Kindrochet and Port-an -Eilean. Lastly, Lude was allocated pews 50-57.[45] Allocation of pews was worked out to suit the requirements of the lairds, their families, tenants and workers. The Robertson heritors of Auchleeks, Blairfettie and Kindrochet, who had been principally involved in preventing the closure of the church, were not given prime positions, but pews in the gallery.

The Reverend G. Calder among others assisted the Blair Atholl minister in the running of Struan church and departed in 1890. He was succeeded by David Fraser McNeill, a probationer, in 1891 and was followed by another probationer, James Silver in 1895.

The church was extensively altered in 1938 when the galleries were removed, the interior subdivided to form a small hall at the back and the seating capacity reduced to about 70. On the rear wall by the communion table is an irregularly-shaped Pictish stone, placed there for safe-keeping in the 1970s. Its most prominent feature is a double disc bisected by a Z-shaped rod, which is one of the most commonly found Pictish symbols. The stone has been dated to around the eighth century.

In the churchyard, a little to the front and right of the church door is a 4-foot high pillar stone, with a simple cross incised on the east and west faces. It is thought to be a very old preaching stone, pre-dating the existence of any formal church building. By the east gable of the church a tombstone erected by "John Crerar in Dalnamein" is a tragic reminder of childhood mortality in the nineteenth century. It bears the names of seven of his children – Alexander who died 6.9.1861 aged 10; Catherine, died 28.9.1861 aged 12; Jessie, died 8.10.1861 aged 3; John, died 2.11.1861 aged 6; Margaret, died 1.12.1861 aged 15; Annie, died 9.12.1861 aged 8 and Donald, died 24.12.1861 aged 17 – all of them from diphtheria within a period of four months.

The essence of the peacefulness of the church at Struan was summed up by the late Reverend Donald Cameron, for many years minister of the combined parish:

. . . On that green knoll at the confluence of the Garry and the Errochty there is a sense of peace and the stillness that speaks to the hearing ear. It is a simple little church – quiet in its surroundings, suited to its environment, blending with one of the beautiful scenes of Scotland – the valley of the Garry.[46]

Similar sentiments have been recorded by people from all over the world in the Visitors Book. Phrases such as "It is such a beautiful and holy place; It's so peaceful; A pilgrimage site, good to be here; I found peace and tranquility", say it all – it is, to quote, a "Very Special Place".

Trinafour Church

Six miles west of Struan church, the way across the Errochty was by means of a fine example of a military road bridge built by General Wade's troops in 1730 and bypassed in the 1950s. It stands below a private chapel built by Edgar William Robertson, twelfth laird of Auchleeks. His wife, Henrietta Matilda, laid the foundation stone on 1 August 1882 using a ceremonial silver trowel now in the Clan Donnachaidh Museum collection at Bruar.

The church is 39 feet in length, inside wall measurement and 21 feet wide, being built to house a congregation of fifty people. It contains two banks of five 8-foot long pews, sufficient to hold five persons per pew, with a centre aisle. There is a small pulpit and a wooden vestry, 11 feet by 7 feet was added in the south-west corner of the church interior in 1967.

The timber belfry contains a bell 12 inches in diameter, inscribed: TO THE GLORY OF GOD. IN LOVING MEMORY OF SARAH M. LEES THE MOTHER OF EDGAR ROBERTSON. J. WARNER & SONS LONDON 1891. It was cast in the Cripplegate Foundry in East London.[47]

Inside the church are one marble and four brass plaques in memory of five successive Auchleeks lairds and their wives who are recorded as follows:

Trinafour church built in1882 with seating for a congregation of fifty people.

Robert Robertson, 9th Laird of Auchleeks.
Born 7 February 1777. Died 23 March 1859.
Wife Bridget born 16 July 1799 died 5 October 1888.

Robert Robertson, 10th Laird.
Born 27 December 1816. Died 6 October 1862.
Emily Robertson, Wife, Born 31 December 1826. Died 14 May 1904.

Robert John Robertson of Auchleeks, 11th Laird.
Born 9 May 1851. Died 4 May 1871.

Edgar William Robertson of Auchleeks 12th Laird.
Born 28 August 1853. Died 17 August 1909.
Wife Henrietta Matilda. Died 4 February 1921.

Earnest Francis Robertson 13th Laird of Auchleeks.
Born 16 July 1856. Died 16 October 1945.
Wife, Jane Maitland, Born 28 July 1855. Died 17 January 1934.

Outside the church, by the east gable, is a cross-shaped gravestone in memory of Harriet Robertson who died in 1897 at the age of 68, the daughter of Robert Robertson, ninth laird of Auchleeks. Later this chapel was incorporated as a place of worship into Blair Atholl and Struan parish but by 1979 services between December and March ceased due to dwindling numbers in the congregation and within a few years services were held "by arrangement". The church finally closed for public worship in 1986 and Donald Mackinlay, Trinafour House, put in an offer for the building and land in December 1987 which was accepted.[48]

References

1. *The History of the Celtic Place-names of Scotland*, Watson
2. PSAS Volume XXIV
3. *Fasti,* Scott
4. SRO CH 2 106/4
5. BCCR Bundle 1127
6. Ibid
7. PSAS Volume XXIV
8. PSAS Volume XIII
9. PSAS Volume I
10. SRO CH 2 430/1
11. SRO CH2 430/2
12. SRO CH 2 106/5
13. Ibid
14. Ibid
15. SRO CH 2 106/6
16. Ibid
17. Ibid
18. Ibid
19. SRO CH 2 430/2
20. Ibid
21. Ibid
22. Ibid
23. Ibid
24. Ibid
25. SRO CH 2 430/3
26. SRO CH 2430/6
27. Ibid
28. BCCR Trunk 33 XVIII
29. BCCR Trunk 59 (4) 523
30. BCCR Bundle 1228
31. BCCR Bundle 1285
32. BCCR Bundle 1228
33. BCCR Trunk 33 XVIII
34. BCCR Bundle 1227
35. SRO CH 2 106/14
36. BCCR Trunk 69 (3) 394
37. BCCR Trunk 69 (3) 420
38. BCCR Trunk 69 (3) 446
39. BCCR Trunk 69 (3) 455
40. BCCR Bundle 1227
41. BCCR Trunk 69 (4) 419
42. BCCR Bundle 1226
43. SRO CH 2 430/8
44. BCCR Trunk 69 (4) 482
45. BCCR Bundle 1227
46. CDA 1955
47. PSAS Volume 122
48. Blair Atholl Session Minutes

six

St Brides Church
Old Blair

This church was dedicated to St Bride or "Brigid the Calm", who has been described as the greatest woman of the Celtic church. Born in Fochart, Dundalk, she joined Kildare, one of the famous Irish religious houses and died around 525, without, it appears, ever having visited Scotland.[1] St Brides fairs were held in Blair, (now Old Blair), twice a year, at Candlemas, (2nd February) for general business and also on the third Wednesday in May for cattle and horse trading.[2]

Around the year 1475, Angus of Islay, son of the Lord of the Isles, raided Atholl to seek revenge on Sir John Stewart, the 1st Earl of Atholl, who had kidnapped his infant son. Along with his second wife, Lady Eleanor Sinclair, he took refuge in St Brides, which was then burnt down, after they had been taken captive and dragged from the altar. On the way back to Islay a great storm blew up during the sea crossing, wrecking some of the galleys and losing much of the Atholl plunder. Believing this to be a sign of divine judgment on him for the sacrilege committed in St Brides, Angus not only liberated his prisoners but barefoot and stripped to the waist, undertook a return pilgrimage with the remaining salvaged spoils to the church, which he rebuilt and then performed a humiliating penance.[3] The coats of arms of John, 4th Earl of Atholl, who died of poisoning and his second wife, Margaret, are on the west outer wall of the Atholl vault.

Little of note has been recorded until 1672 when an act of parliament was passed in favour of John, 2nd Murray Earl of Atholl:

The arms of John, 4th Earl of Atholl and his wife, Margaret, on the outer wall of the vault of St Brides church.

> Anent a supplication to the King's Maistie be Johne Earle of Atholl . . . having donated ane considerable part of the stipend with the manse and gleib, and in respect of the vacancie thereof, there being no present incumbent to serve the cuir, the said kirk is altogidder ruinous, and if the same be not presentlie repaired will altogidder decay. The King's Maistie with advice and consent of his estates of Parliament doe hereby give warrand to uplift the vacand stipend of the said paroche of Blair for the year 1672 and to apply the samyn for repairing the said Kirk.[4]

Extensive repairs were carried out and there are no records of further renovations for the next fifty years.

In addition to the Atholl family, the interior of the church was allocated to the principal families in the area bearing the name of Stewart, much in the same way that the church at Struan was the burial place for Robertsons. In St Brides it was the Stewarts of Urrard and Orchil who exercised their right of burial there. The oldest date that can be deciphered on a gravestone is 1516, marking a resting place for the Stewarts of Urrard.

An isolated headstone behind the north wall of the church marks the final resting place of three skeletons which were found in the castle in 1869 during the course of extensive alterations and additions. When excavating beneath the wine cellar, formerly the stables prior to 1744, a skeleton was found eighteen inches below the floor and two more on the following day. These were apparently of young men with no marks of violence on the remains. At first it was thought they had been part of the garrison during the siege of 1746 but there were no casualties recorded from that incident. Another possibility is that they were from Captain Witte's parliamentary troops who were killed during a skirmish with the Earl of Atholl's forces in 1654.[5]

Neil Stewart from Invervack, an Edinburgh merchant, died in 1790 and the epitaph on his tombstone reads:

> Although the worms devour my skin
> and waste my growing flesh
> yet God will raise them up again
> and clothe them all afnosh [afresh]

Another headstone commemorates a visitor, William Butterell from Doncaster, who died while travelling through the district. "During a journey on commercial pursuits he was taken ill at this place on 16.8.1818 and died 28.8.1818, aged 50, leaving a wife and only son".

1727 Repairs

Presbytery plans for repairing Struan and St Brides churches and manse were considered in 1727 and Adam Brown, mason, gave an estimate for work requiring to be done in St Brides:[6]

		£ Scots
Item:	Downtaking and rebuilding north stair and for pinning, harling the south stair	13. 0. 0
Item:	Building up foundation and putting up other places needful about the kirk	4. 0. 0
Item:	Winning skews, squaring them and putting them on	6. 0. 0
Item:	For enlarging the fore window	4.13. 2
Item:	50 bolls of lime for the use of the church at a merk a boll	33. 6. 8
Mason work		£60.19.10
Item:	Repairing Kirkyard dykes	£13. 0. 0

Patrick McInnes and John Lauder, wrights, estimated as follows:[7]

		£ Scots
Item:	Raising boards and mending sarking using 16 dales at 9 shillings a piece	7. 4. 0
Item:	Supporting cuples above isle and mending a cuple below joists	9. 0. 0
Item:	500 double plenshions at 8 shillings per 100 for use in the kirk	2. 0. 0
Item:	A dozen double garron nails	12. 0
Item:	Setting up scaffolds, raising the old sarking and making new and mending a broken cuple	6.13. 4
Item:	Glazing 5 windows in the east gable and enlarged window in the loft, amounts to 69 feet 6 inches at 4 shillings and 6 pence each foot	15.12. 9
Item:	Making a new pulpit	9. 0. 0
Item:	Nails, hinges and other iron work for the pulpit	3. 0. 0
Item:	Workmanship of pulpit	12. 0. 0
Item:	Scaffolding , dales and supports	15. 0. 0
Wright work		£80. 2. 1

Extract from "A Plan of Blair in Atholl by Chas. Esplen from Thomas Winters 1744" which clearly shows St Brides church with a bell tower and the adjacent manse.

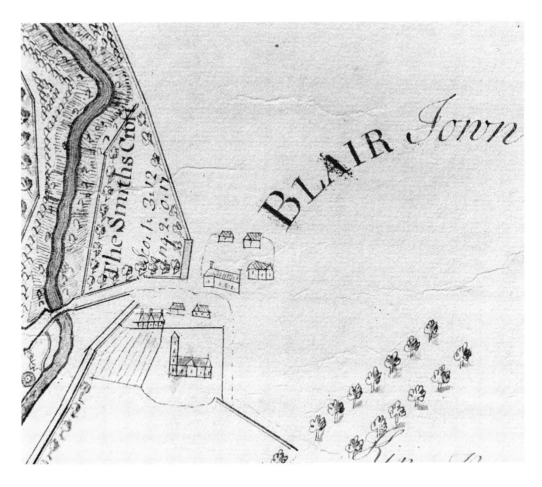

The estimate from the slaters, John McCraw and Andrew McMillan, was as follows:[8]

		£ Scots
Item:	500 skeille	4. 0. 0
Item:	Ground meal	1. 0. 0
Item:	800 single plenshions	2. 8. 0
Item:	Workmanship	36. 0. 0
Item:	2 bolls of lime for rigging	1. 6. 8
Item:	4 foot of Rigging Stone	16. 0
Slater work		£45.10. 8

The sum total of renovation work for St Brides in 1727, including the kirkyard, came to £199.12.7 Scots, equivalent to about £17 Sterling. The estimate tells us that the east gable contained five windows, the evidence of which is still visible, as is the enlarged window in the gallery.

Estimates for the steeple (bell tower) of St Brides were as follows:
Mason Work: [9]

		£ Scots
Item:	Winning stones, levelling walls, making up foundations	16. 0. 0

Wright Work

		£ Scots
Item:	for making 28 joists	28. 0. 0
Item:	Sarking the roof and making roof windows, 80 dales	32. 0. 0
Item:	5 dozen garron nails and 1500 double plenshions	9. 0. 0
Item:	Workmanship, binding sarking, joisting to support the bell, roof windows and ladder	24. 0. 0
		£93. 0. 0

Slater Work

		£ Scots
Item:	2000 skaillie	16. 0. 0
Item:	Ground meal, 2,600 nails at 6 shillings a hundred	11.10. 0
Item:	2 roods and 2 ells work at £10 per rood	20.10. 0
		£48. 0. 0

The total cost of repairing the bell tower came to £157 Scots. The substantial footings of this are still clearly visible at the west entrance of the church.

1742 Repairs
As with Struan these repairs lasted for under twenty years before major renovations were needed. Estimates were again obtained from masons, joiners and slaters by 25 November 1742, the same tradesmen being employed for Struan church:[10]
Mason Work

		£ Scots
Item:	Taking down and rebuilding 26 foot long and 18 foot high of the back wall and 27 foot long and 16 foot high of the forewall east of the isle and of the forewall west	

		£ Scots
	of the isle, in all 3½ roods at £18 per rood	63. 0. 0
Item:	Pinning and dressing 100 foot of fence	5. 0. 0
Item:	Repairing the foundations of the bell tower, levelling the top fitting for the roof	14. 0. 0
Item:	Pinning and harling Kirk Steeple and Isle	48. 0. 0
Item:	Quarrying steps for two stairs and building same	25. 4. 0
Item:	100 bolls of lime for building	60. 0. 0
Item:	60 bolls of lime for pinning and harling	36. 0. 0
Item:	Quarrying what is needed	10. 0. 0
Mason work		£261. 4. 0
Item:	Carrying Stone	15. 0. 0
Item:	Carriage of Lime	8. 0. 0
Item:	Carriage of Sand	24. 0. 0
Carriage Costs		£47. 0. 0

Wright Work[11]

		£ Scots
Item:	136 trees	136. 0. 0
Item:	530 dales at 8d ster. per dale	212. 0. 0
Item:	Mending floors of the two galleries and 4 doors, 24 dales at 8d ster. per dale	9. 12. 0
Item:	Making a window in the foreside and 5 little window frames, 6 dales	2. 8. 0
Item:	7,500 double plenshions at £1.1.4 per 1,000	8. 0. 0
Item:	1,000 double flooring nails	25. 5. 0
Item:	Taking down the roof and erecting scaffolding	18. 0. 0
Item:	Binding, setting up and sarking roof	68. 0. 0
Item:	Binding, setting up and sarking the steeple roof	30. 0. 0
Item:	Repairing floor of the two galleries and making four double doors and one door case and a big window case and casement with four little window frames for glass	32. 0.0
Wright work		£541. 5. 0
Item:	Carriage for dales and trees	£ 96. 0. 0

Slater Work[12]

		£ Scots
Item:	8 roods of slate work at £10 per rood	80. 0. 0
Item:	Furnishing of slates for 5 roods of above at £8 per rood	40. 0. 0
Item:	Taking down the old slates	12. 0. 0
Item:	16,000 nails and 20 foot of rigan stone	42. 0. 0
Item:	1 rood and 30 ells at £18 per rood	33. 0. 0
Item:	Nails for steeple and mending isle and furnishing slates	16. 0. 0
Slate work		£223. 0. 0
Item:	For carriage 330 horse at 20d per piece and rigan stone and nails	£111.16. 0

Glasswork[13]

	£ Scots
Estimate of Thomas Clark, glazier for glasswork	£5.13. 0

St Brides church in 1870. The former Old Blair inn, now a private house, is on the right.

Although now long roofless, much of the shell of this old church remains. The blocked-up window apertures in the east gable and the large gap for the east gallery window are still to be seen. The empty doorways to the galleries at first-floor level in the north and south walls remain as does the stonework base of the old gallery stair on the outside of the north wall. There are four window apertures in the south wall, one of which was for the west gallery. A fine stone arch leads off the south-east corner to an area over the vault where the Atholl family sat in semi-privacy. This is opposite a blocked-in door with a window above in the north wall, presumably the minister's door leading to the pulpit, with a window for light.

Ministers
Walter Stewart became minister of the combined parish in 1614 and died between October 1643 and April 1647 when Colin Campbell of Tulliepowrie in Strathtay was appointed his successor. He was the fifth son of Archibald Campbell of Laggansgiach and Christian Robertson, whose father was Alexander Robertson of Inchmagranachan. He graduated from St Andrews University in 1640, having completed his degree a year earlier than usual. Three years later he was ordained as minister of Killin parish, thereafter serving in the army as a chaplain and came to Blair Atholl in November 1647. In the following year he married Jean, daughter of James Stewart of Fincastle and on 14 June 1649 her father granted them the five merk land of Easter Tulliepowrie. The Earl of Atholl granted him the lands of Fincastle, Allean, Clune and Edintian with its shieling called Allt na Saobaidh in 1657. He died in 1667 and his position as minister was taken by his oldest son, Robert.[14]

Like his father, Robert Campbell, born in 1642, graduated from St Andrews and was ordained in 1667. He married Anne, eldest daughter of James Murray, minister of Logierait, in 1675 and died in 1699.[15] Colin Campbell's brother Robert was minister of Moulin from 1647 to 1668, when he refused to accept prelacy and was removed from the presbytery.[16]

The Reverend Duncan Stewart was born in 1756 and gained an MA from

Glasgow University in 1775. He was appointed as minister of Dunoon parish in 1686 until 1690 when he was deposed by the Act of Parliament which restored presbyterian ministers. A Jacobite sympathiser, he came to Blair Atholl around 1700 and in February 1716 he was stated to have:

> . . . intruded into the kirks of Blair Atholl and Struan, these many years bygone, never having prayed to King George but only in general terms for the Sovereign, having read the proclamation for the Thanksgiving for the Pretender's safe arrival on 22 Jan. last, having also a great hand in influencing the people to rebellion and read all the proclamations emitted by the Earl of Mar.[17]

He was a literary man and his best-known work, *A Short Historical and Genealogical Account of the Royal Family of Scotland from Kenneth II*, was to become the acknowledged authority of the time on that subject. He appears to have been a man of means since he gave money to the Marquis of Atholl in 1703 for travelling expenses to London to receive his dukedom from Queen Anne! As a reward for this, the new duke granted him a feu in 1708 for the land of Strathgarry and half the Kirrachan Shieling for 4,631 merks (£257 Sterling) and an annual payment of 33 merks (£1.16.8 Sterling):

> . . . All and hail the 5 merk land of Strathgarie and a pendicle thereof called ffuarchasach with houses, biggings, yards, tofts, crofts, grassings, sheallings, meadow, pasturages, woods and fishings. . . .[18]

Thus the Reverend Duncan Stewart became the first Stewart laird of Strathgarry and he died sometime between 1728 and March 1730.

Dunkeld Presbytery was determined to oust this intruder but out of loyalty to Duncan Stewart the duke forbade this and although summoned to Dunkeld to account for his actions he never appeared. He thus remained in Blair Atholl until 1715 when, on account of his inciting support from the pulpit for the Jacobite cause, the duke withdrew his support and agreed he should be prosecuted by the sheriff. However there is evidence that as late as 1728 he was still in the parish as the minister, Robert Bisset, wrote to presbytery informing them that:

> Mr Duncan Stewart who kept a meeting house in his paroch being dead, the people attend ordinances pretty well and hopes that if a stop were put to their getting of another to keep a meeting that they would all generally attend ordinances there.[19]

This meant that over all those years since the duke had withdrawn his support, Duncan Stewart remained in the district with a substantial number of adherents, possibly meeting in a small chapel near Aldclune.

By his first wife, Anna, daughter of Aeneas Mclaine, minister of Kilfinan he had two sons, Alexander and Donald. His second wife, Janet McCalman, produced several children, and she was determined that Allan, her first-born, should be on the same level materially as his half-brothers. She indulged in the "undignified occupation" of distilling illicit whisky in her back garden and was so successful in this enterprise that with the proceeds she was able to buy the Innerhadden estate and Allan became its first Stewart laird.[20]

Robert Bisset, born in 1696 and son of James Bisset, clerk of the Regality Court of Atholl, was ordained in Kirkmichael in 1720. He was transferred to

Blair Atholl in 1726 and died on 17 February 1739. His eldest son, Thomas, became minister of Logierait.[21]

The Reverend Duncan Stewart's grandson, Alexander, who was also third laird of Strathgarry, was born in 1712 and later studied at Edinburgh University. The Duke of Atholl considered proposing him as minister for Blair Atholl but "judged it convenient to delay it for two years that the vacant stipend might be employed in repairing the fabrick of that church". The Reverend Adam Ferguson advised him not to delay the appointment because:

> 26 July 1740
> If this be put off for a year longer his modest work may influence others to call him elsewhere and his circumstances oblige him to accept of the invitation by which will be lost our opportunity to have an agreeable countryman there. A proposal was made to him to engage to be helper to Mr Campbell at Weem which he discreetly refused because I had acquainted him with your friendly design to have him at Blair. . . . I know Mr Stewart so well that I verily believe he is the fittest for that place of any of my acquaintances.[22]

Alexander Stewart was ordained as minister of Blair Atholl parish on 6 May 1741 and remained its minister until he died in July 1780. He was a distinguished Gaelic scholar and pulpit orator. He married Isobel, daughter of John Robertson of Lude in 1742 and his eldest son, Duncan, became minister of Balquidder, having been proposed by the Duke of Atholl. Alexander wrote to the duke to thank him for his assistance:

> 22 April 1722
> I beg leave in the most respectful manner to thank Your Grace for offering to present my son to the vacancy in Balquidder. I am advised he accepts the favour with gratitude. He is still hoping that when a more comfortable settlement casts up Your Grace will remember him.[23]

Alexander Stewart's successor was James MacLagan, born in 1728, the son of a farmer in Ballechin in Strathtay. He completed his education at St Andrews, became an ordained minister in 1760 and started as a missionary at Amulree church after which he became army chaplain to the 42nd Foot. He was awarded the freedom of the City of Glasgow in 1776 and in 1780, Thomas Bissett, the Atholl factor, acting on behalf of the duke, presented his credentials to Dunkeld Presbytery as the most suitable candidate for the Blair Atholl church vacancy. This was accepted and he came to Blair Atholl on 29 March 1781.

James MacLagan composed the Gaelic words for the music of "The Garb of Old Gaul", composed by General Sir John Reid of Straloch, as well as translating part of the Bible into Gaelic for the Scottish Society for the Propagation of Christian Knowledge. In 1792 he compiled the entry for Blair Atholl and Struan parish for the First Statistical Account of Scotland, which was edited by Sir John Sinclair. His collection of Gaelic manuscripts is in Glasgow University archives.[24]

Poor Relief

Until 1751 parishes were responsible for administering relief to their own poor. From then on the heritors in each parish held that responsibility in theory but usually acted through the kirk session.

There was a combined meeting of heritors and the kirk session on 17 May 1744 to draw up a plan for assisting the poor "in this time of Dearth", which reached the following conclusions:

1. That lists of the begging poor be prepared for the meeting the following Monday;
2. That the lists be purged, the non-indigent cast out and badges given to the Indigent . . . and some method employed to restrain the non Indigent from begging;
3. That the poor of other parishes be sent home to their own parishes . . . and a proper person employed at the expense of the parish to rid the parish of such vagabonds;
4. That the session raise the maximum funds as quickly as possible to supply members of the poor who were unable to travel and purchase lint to be spun by those who can spin, for which they will be paid in meal.[25]

As parish minister, James MacLagan was well aware of the dire circumstances of the poor as this letter to the duke shows:

9 July 1783
The number of poor needing supply amounted to 180 and each of these would require five firlots of meal to maintain him till the middle of September when the new crop will probably relieve. This amounts to 225 bolls. The funds we have in hand amount to eleven bolls after which remain still unprovided 214 bolls.[26]

Other problems of the poor and limited funds to support them in ways other than food, took up much of the Reverend MacLagan's time as this letter to the duke shows:

29 February 1800
I have enquired of Mr Robertson of Lude [General William Robertson] what is known about Robert Scot and find that Lude turned him and his brother out of his land in 1794 because they would not be volunteers [The Loyal Clan Donnachie Volunteers, formed by the General]. That then Robert Scot took a cot-house in Tirinie where he shewed the first signs of insanity. . . . Unfortuneatley he will come upon this parish unless his having become a soldier (they say in 46th Regt) . . . endeavour to get him into a correction house or Bedlam which they say may be done for a small sum – our parish funds are at present very unequal to such a burden, there being very little in the Poor's box, tho' there is much need for it. And should the principal be broken there will be nothing for the poor, our Sunday collections when the family of Atholl is not here, being a mere trifle.[27]

Later that year he wrote again to the duke:

31 July 1800
I at this time express the lively sense I have of Your Grace's judicious and humane exertions in supplying the populous county of Perth with bread in these distressing times. As well as my most grateful thanks for the kindness shown by Your Grace to the poor part of the flock of which I have the honour

St Brides church from the east.

to be pastor, of whom I believe many would starve had it not been for the supply of oats and wheat meal you brought to the country at such an expence of money and labour. . . . I glory in Your Grace's having acted in a manner worthy of the first man in Perthshire.[28]

That this problem was still acute in 1801, is recorded in a report by the minister to a committee of heritors:

The funds of the poor are extremely low. I hope the heritors of the parish will assess themselves in five shillings on every hundred pounds of valued rent. They may have to be collected by the school master and given to Mr MacLagan.[29]

Kirk Session
At the session meeting on 26 March 1719, the session clerk, James Murray, asked for a "standing fee yearly" as his reasoning was:

. . . that he was the first session clerk in this paroch who wrote and kept the Minutes of the Session since the Revolution and probably since the Reformation (for there were no Minutes of Sessions kept in this Paroch formerly, or if there were, the Minister and Session who are now, never see them.)[30]

The post of beadle, or church officer, at that time, not only included attending on the minister and being responsible for church and churchyard maintenance, but also summoning and escorting defaulters to session meetings. The question of paying him for doing so arose at the meeting on 26 February 1719:

This day the Session considering the vast pains of Beddall [Robert Gow] is at in summoning delinquents to the Session, enacted that he should have ane half merk Scots (6/8d) for each person he should summond from those that employed him, and if the Session employed him, that he should be payd by those whom he summond if they were convicted . . . but if the Session desired him upon a summons and that the crime alledged could not be proven, then the Session was not to pay him, seeing he was their Servant, and had a yearly allowance from them.[31]

Robert Gow gave up the post of beadle on 22 November 1719, his place being taken by Donald Gow, with special rulings concerning burials being laid down at the meeting on 29 December that year:

. . . The Session appoints Donald Gow their Beddall to prevent all debates that may arise and mistakes with respect to buriall places within the Church or Church yard, to take inspection of the ground peculiar to each family who have right to bury in the said place and to dig the graves for which he is to have 6/3 Scots for every man or woman's grave digging and 3/3 Scots for every child or infant's grave digging. In order to which, the Session is to keap up two speads and a shovell for that end.[32]

There was also the ongoing necessity of keeping up the number of elders in the kirk session and "A List of Elders newly chosen out of the List given in as was appointed, by 18th June inst." was as follows:

Blair 22 June 1722
     John Scot in Tennendrie; Robert Moon in Borannich; John Robertson McWilliam Roy in Bohespick; Mr James Robertson in Auchlix; John Duff in Dalnamin; James Robertson in Clunes; Angus Robertson in Pitagowan; Donald McPharlane in Calabruar; George Ritchie in Baluain; Donald Stewart in Urrardbeg; Robert Steuart in Blairuachdar; Charles Conacher in Blair; Grigor Murray Taxman of Katherine's Mill [Mill of Blair];William Steuart in Innerslanie; Duncan Campbell in Drumnabeachan; William Steuart in Nether Campsie; Patrick Steuart in Little Lude; Patrick McGlashan in Wester Monzie; George Steuart att the Miln of Kincraigie; Finlay Robertson in Strathgroie; Charles McLaren in Kilmavennock; Malcolm Steuart in Tulloch; Donald Steuart in Pitaldonich; Alexander McLauchlane in Fanvuick.[33]

The session dealt with a variety of offences such as all types of sexual immorality, illegitimacy, breaches of the peace and observance of the Lord's Day, defamation of character, breach of promise of marriage and so on. Depending on the nature of the offence, defaulters were rebuked before the session, had to show their repentance publicly in church, were fined and often had to find someone to put up a sum of money as a guarantee of their future good behaviour.

     There are several cases of a man who had applied to have a child baptised but been found guilty of a misdemeanour and was not to be allowed "to hold his Child in baptism:"

Blair Atholl 29 September 1719
     Donald McLaren walker at the walk miln of Blair Atholl (who was alledged to be guilty of fishing on the Lord's Day) and therefore would not be permitted

a while ago to hold up his Child to Baptism but behoved to find a Sponsor, being called – compeared and being asked how he came to be weet and wieding [wading] the water so timous in the morning on the Lords Day, he said it was for other ends he did weide the water so timous, than to fish. And being desired by the Session to pay his Baptism monie he positively denyd, seeing he was not permitted to hold his own child to Baptism.[34]

Blair Atholl 10 April 1720

This day Donald Robertson in Dachinlialish in Stragroie being immediately summond and cited, compeared, who was seeking the benefit of Baptism to his Child but the said Donald being on a Sabbath Day a while ago miserably drunk and that before several of the congregation . . . he would stand before the Congregation against Sabbath next and give Signs of his Sorrow for such a Crime and be publickly rebuked for it . . . and that he would get ane oyther honest man free of any Scandall to hold his Child to Baptism. . . .[35]

Blair Atholl 17 April 1720

This day Donald Robertson, Tinkler in Dachinlialash in Stragroie was rebuked before the Congregation for being Drunk on a Sabbath day and drinking all the time of the Sermon a while agoe.[36]

Offenders committing breaches of observance of the Sabbath and fast days were also called to account:

Blair Atholl 1 May 1720

. . . no travellers should travel with baggage on the Sabbath day, that their baggage should be taken from them till Sabbath was over. And that those without a reasonable excuse absent, or stay away from Divine Service on the Lord's Day should be fined. The Session appoints to send to the Clerk of the Court to get ane Extract of the Act, and it should be read publickly in the church here, for preventing the like in the future. . . .[37]

11 April 1744

. . . Susan McGlashan wife to Donald Robertson in Easter Kindrochett being summoned to answer for breach of Sabbath by leading a horse with a load of baggage upon him from the Boat of Apersuanie [Woodend Ferry] to the said Donald's house. . . .[38]

15 April 1744

Alex Gow in Blair made his appearance before the Congregation for his breach of the fast day . . . [he] acknowledged he was guilty in breaking the late fast . . . by Musick and Dancing in his house . . . and James Gow taylor in Invervack confessed that he danced in Alex Gows house that fast day, being rebuked by the Session and to consign a bill of five pounds Scots as security of his future good behaviour.[39]

Instances of acccusations of invoking evil on neighbours have been recorded:

Blair Atholl 29 May 1720

This day Elspet Robertson in this town being delated as one guilty of horrible Imprecations on James McLaren in this town and [he] being just now become very sick very shortly thereafter and so as yet still continues, so that his right hand is greatly swollen and vehemently tormenting him and he otherways very Sick so that he is liker to die than live; therefore the Session appoints her to be summoned against Sabbath next and diligent enquiry to be made if any heard her imprecating the said McLaren. . . .[40]

Strowan 14 October 1744

Margaret Robertson, spouse to Neill Stewart in Haugh of Easter Invervack being summoned for Imprecating and wishing ill to Robert Robertson in Milntoun of Invervack and his family, being called, compeared and was seriously exhorted and rebuked sessionally for her heinous crime and enjoining her to have a more decent and Christian behaviour for the future, was dismissed.[41]

21 May 1749

John Robertson in Wester Balhuain being interrogate if he, when he made charms to John Tossich's cow in Wester Monzie, said that the Witch in the Toun end did harm to the said cow, denyed that he ever uttered such.[42]

In this case, John Robertson is said to have implied that Elspeth McLauchlan (who lived in the same settlement) was guilty of witchcraft, although he denied it.

Concern was also shown about events which caused personal loss to parishioners, through no fault of their own:

Blair Atholl 18 January 1761

There was an application made to the Session on behalf of Alex McLauchlane in Brae of Lude who had his horse in harvest killed by a thunder-clap, he hardly escaping himself being just beside said horse, for a collection to be made at both the churches in this parish, in order to help him in buying another, to keep him from being a burden upon the parish. . . .[43]

23 July 1761

An intimation was given by the appointment of the Kirk Session of Blair for a collection against Sabbath next here, for the relief of George Stewart in Easter Invervack [Stewartston] who had his house and all his furniture therein lately burnt by accidental fire. . . .[44]

St Brides graveyard in 1870.

2 August 1761

. . . collected for the said George Stewart £22.5.10 Scots. . . .[45]

There also seems to have been a standard fine for arriving late for your own, or a relative's wedding:

Blair Atholl 10 January 1762

John MacLauchlane in Brae of Lude was fined in two shillings Ster. for being too late in coming at his Daughter's marriage, of which one shilling Ster. was left with himself to give to any poor object he sees most needful. . . .[46]

Professor Robin Barbour, interim moderator of Tenandry church, preaching in front of St Brides in 1989 during the tercentenary commemoration service for the Battle of Killiecrankie.

7 March 1762

Alexander Stewart in Tressaitte paid in two shillg. Ster. for his coming too late to marry and four shillings Scots was collected at his marriage. . . .[47]

Minor church repairs and the supply of Communion elements and coffins for strangers appear from time to time in the minutes:

Blair Atholl 20 September 1747

Alex Gow Senior in Blair gave in an account due to him of the Session several years ago of four shillings Ster. for repairing the Quire, repentance stool, seats and bars, which the Session ordered to be payd him presently. . . .[48]

13 October 1771

. . . The Session appointed 16sh Ster for coffins and dead cloths for the two women that were lost upon a rapid burn this side of Minigaig going home to the north from Lothian shearing.[49]

The greatest part of the session's time in the eighteenth century was taken up in dealing with allegations of all forms of sexual immorality, too numerous to mention. Offenders often delayed, or were unwilling to appear before the session, which then laid down strict rules to enforce this:

Blair Atholl 13 September 1719

A List of the persons in Blair Atholl Paroch that are guilty of fornication and will not answer the Session but are Contumacious and will not subject themselves to Church Discipline tho' they have been 3 severall times summoned by the Beddall . . . the persons are Contumacious . . . therefore these are requiring the Ground Officer to go along with two of the elders or church officers and charge them to come and give obedience to the Minister and Session, which if they refuse and continue Contumacious, that the said officer charge and summond them to the first regality court thereafter at the Instance of the said Kirk Session and procurator fiscall of court. . . .[50]

Early Travellers

Daniel Defoe was one of the early travellers from England to tour Scotland and in the account of his 1769 journey he portrayed the church as "a poor old kirk, the pews all broken down, doors open, full of dirt, where the minister preached once a week". In 1811 Garnett described it a "mean-looking church resembling an English barn" while Dorothy Wordsworth was kinder, saying it was the most interesting object she saw at Blair, "shaded with trees".

Burial Vault

There is a burial vault on the south side of the church, above which was the Blair Castle family pew, directly in front of the pulpit. According to the Reverend Dr Alexander Irvine, a duchess of Atholl was buried here and he claims this in some hand-written notes he prepared on the history of St Brides in 1864:

> Now it is certain that a Duchess of Atholl was buried in the vault and there are persons now alive who remember seeing the hatchment put upon the occasion over the arch within which was the family pew.[51]

That this was indeed a "duchess" is speculative and the cryptic comment "never" scribbled in the margin of the minister's notes, by the 7th duke, would indicate that this was untrue.

Viscount Claverhouse, "Bonnie Dundee" who fell at the Battle of Killiecrankie in 1689, was interred here. About a hundred years later, General William Robertson of Lude was informed that the vault had been opened and that "the body of a man who had been buried in his armour was discovered". He hastened to the church only to find that the grave-digger had disposed of most of the armour to a band of passing tinkers, who wanted it for the sake of its brass rivets. He was just in time to rescue part of the helmet and also the breast-plate which is now preserved in Blair Castle.[52]

On the date of the bi-centenary of the Battle of Killiecrankie in 1889, the 7th duke unveiled an inscribed memorial tablet in honour of Viscount Claverhouse on the inner face of the south wall of the church, beside the vault:

The memorial tablet put up in St Brides church by the 7th Duke of Atholl in honour of Viscount Claverhouse who was buried here after the Battle of Killiecrankie.

Within the vault beneath
are interred the remains of
JOHN GRAHAM OF
CLAVERHOUSE
VISCOUNT OF DUNDEE
who fell at the Battle of Killiecrankie
27 July 1689 aged 46
This memorial is placed here by
JOHN 7th DUKE OF ATHOLE KT
1889

A possible cresset stone with twelve hollows for holding oil.

A service to commemorate the tercentenary of the battle was held outside the church on Thursday 27 July 1989, when over 200 people attended. The service was conducted by the Right Reverend Alastair Haggart, formerly Bishop of Edinburgh and Primus of the Scottish Episcopal Church, whose theme was "Healing the Memories". A service was also held beside the memorial cairn on the battlefield, jointly conducted by Professor (now Sir) Robin Barbour, interim moderator at Tenandry church; the Reverend James Duncan, minister of Blair Atholl and Struan and Michael Hare-Duke, Episcopal Bishop of St Andrews, Dunkeld and Dunblane.

The vault was opened in January 1864 to prepare it for the interment of George, 6th Duke of Atholl, thus creating a precedent, as the 1st to 5th dukes are all interred in the crypt in Dunkeld Cathedral. The Reverend Dr Irvine witnessed the scene:

The floor of the vault, which had not been paved, was covered to the depth of some feet, with a promiscuous mass of bones, fragments of coffins, earth and stones. This must have arisen from the rubbish in this area of the church having been shovelled into the openings of the vault and which, descending on the stair, the steps of which it almost entirely concealed, covered over or became mixed with the remains of those who had been buried in it. It will give some idea of the accumulation of bones to state that thirty two skulls, most of them quite entire, were dug out, besides fragments of others which had mouldered away. Of the skulls, some had the marks of sword cuts which had healed, while of those that were fractured, it was difficult to say whether they had been broken before or after burial.[53]

After removing the debris, the vault floor was flagged and the arch over it was described as being in "excellent preservation". The bones that had been retrieved were gathered together and deposited in a coffin which was placed in a corner of the vault, where a metal plate recording the second interment was inserted in the wall.

After the death of the 6th Duke, a private service was conducted on Saturday 23 January 1864 by the Reverend Court Granville, the duke's brother-in law, in the Horn Hall, now part of the main entrance to the castle. Prayers were offered up by the Reverend Dr Alexander Irvine in front of the castle for those attending outside, while prayers were also offered on the upper avenue by the Reverend Duncan Campbell, minister of Moulin.

As the procession moved off, forty nine rounds (one for every year of the duke's age) were fired at minute intervals by the artillery of the Atholl Highlanders. The coffin was borne, shoulder high by relays of ten men of the Highlanders, led by the regiment and its pipers. The interment service was conducted within the ruins of St Brides as the minister recorded:

> . . . in whose vault, amid the deepest silence unbroken save by the usual military honours after the coffin had been lowered to its resting place, was left all that was mortal of George, Sixth Duke of Athole.[54]

A white marble memorial tablet, depicting the 6th Duke, by Sir John Steele, RSA was afterwards placed in the one-time dukes' pew over the vault. There is a smaller memorial tablet to his widow, Duchess Anne, who died at Dunkeld on 18 May 1897 and was interred beside him.

In the corner of the church between the east gable and the south wall are three small inscribed tablets with the dates: 4 April 1875; 16 July 1876 and 4 November 1877. These simple stones are in memory of three stillborn sons of the 7th duke and duchess. Nearby stands an ancient stone slab with twelve small incised cup marks, which might have been a cresset stone containing oil for lighting purposes.

The 7th duchess, Louisa, died during a train journey to Milan in July 1902. She had expressed a wish not to be buried in St Brides vault and her burial therefore took place in a new cemetery on the south-east side of Hercules Park, off the main drive. John, Marquis of Tullibardine, her eldest son, was born in 1869 but survived only a few hours. He was first buried in St Brides but the coffin was transferred to the new burial ground alongside his mother.[55]

The burial enclosure for the Atholl family, adjacent to St Brides Church.

John, the 7th duke, died in January 1917 and three days later a private funeral service for relatives, friends and tenants was held at the front door of the castle, after which the coffin was borne by Atholl Highlanders to the new burial ground. His eldest daughter, Lady Dorothea, who died in 1937, was also buried there, as was John George, the 8th duke, who died on 15 March 1942.

In September 1955, his brother the 9th duke, always known as Lord James, acquired legal possession of St Brides and its churchyard. He enclosed a family burying site with iron railings, a little to the west of the church, between it and the Banvie and had all the coffins from the private cemetery south of Hercules Park re-interred there.[56] He too, was buried there in 1957, as was the 10th duke, George Iain, in March 1996 – possibly the last great ducal funeral, honoured by its own Atholl Highlanders to be seen in Old Blair.

Rain in Atholl

The broken kirk is dank and green,
The hill wind sobs, the fir tree weeps,
And a whittret, slim and lank and lean,
Slinks by where Clavers sleeps.

From the grim mist where Urrard lies
The birches burst like armed men
And the wild cateran -tempest cries
The slogan down the glen

The clouds, like gathering eagles wing
Above Garry pools, awhirl
With brown blood shed when James was king.

Here smiles a snowdrop girl

J B Salmond

Chapelton

About two miles up the River Banvie from St Brides there is a large area of depopulation, bounded by a substantial dry-stone dyke and two streams, one of which has the ancient name of Allt an t-Seapail (*Stream of the Chapel*) indicating the presence of some bygone place of worship. This is Chapelton, once a large settlement which contains the footings of at least nine buildings, two kilns and associated enclosures. A rental dated 2 January 1713 mentions "the shealling of Rienchapel", indicating its use as a place of summer pasture. It is recorded in the parochial registers from 1718 to 1736 as "Chappel", while it is marked in Roy's military survey of 1747 to 1755 as "Chapel". The last reference to "Chaple" appears in a rental of 1783. By this time it was also appearing in documents as Balinchappel and Balintepail, although James Stobie shows it in 1780 in its modern spelling. There are no references to any chapel building there in the Blair Castle archives or any other manuscript sources so far consulted. Fieldwork has also failed to reveal any evidence of such a building, so it may be concluded that any place of worship there dates far back into the past, probably before written documentation, with evidence surviving only in the name of the stream.

References

1. *St Bride*, Wilkie
2. *New Statistical Account . . .*
3. CAT Volume I
4. BCCR Bundle 224
5. CAT Volume 5
6. SRO CH 2 106/5
7. Ibid
8. Ibid
9. Ibid
10. SRO CH 2 106/6
11. Ibid
12. Ibid
13. Ibid
14. DPD, Hunter
15. *Fasti*, Scott
16. DPD, Hunter
17. *Fasti*, Scott
18. BCCR AC Volume 1
19. SRO CH 2 106/5
20. Strathgarry Papers
21. *Fasti*, Scott
22. BCCR Trunk 46 (13) 96
23. BCCR Trunk 54 (3) 84
24. *Fasti*, Scott
25. SRO CH 2 430/2
26. BCCR Trunk 65 (4) 107
27. BCCR Trunk 48 (1) 222
28. BCCR Trunk 48 (1) 134
29. BCCR Trunk 48 (2) 40
30. SRO CH 2 430/1
31. Ibid
32. Ibid
33. Ibid
34. Ibid
35. Ibid
36. Ibid
37. Ibid
38. SRO CH 2 430/2
39. Ibid
40. SRO CH 2 430/1
41. SRO CH 2 430/2
42. Ibid
43. SRO CH 2 430/3
44. Ibid
45. Ibid
46. Ibid
47. Ibid
48. SRO CH 2 430/2
49. SRO CH 2 430/3
50. SRO CH 2 430/1
51. BCCR Bundle 224
52. Ibid
53. Ibid
54. Ibid
55. CAT Volume 5
56 CAT Volume 6

ADVOCATION & INTERDICT,

Colonel ALEXANDER ROBERTSON of Strowan, and OTHERS, Heritors of the United Parishes of Blair-Athole and Strowan;

AGAINST

The Reverend PRESBYTERY of DUNKELD, &c.

GEORGE, &c.—WHEREAS it is humbly meant and shewn to us by our lovites Colonel ALEXANDER ROBERTSON of Strowan, Lieutenant-General WILLIAM ROBERTSON of Lude, ALEXANDER REID, Esq. of Blairphettie, and the Reverend JOHN ROBERTSON, his factor; DUNCAN ROBERTSON, Esq. of Auchleeks, and Doctor ALEXANDER ROBERTSON of Alexandria, his acting trustee; PATRICK ROBERTSON, Esq. of Trinafour, and JAMES ROBERTSON, Esq. of Kindrochit, all heritors in the united parishes of Blair-Athole and Strowan,—THAT, in the month of September last, without any previous

KEGGIE, *Printer, Old Assembly Close.*

Advocation and interdict concerning the attempted suppression of Struan church in 1820.

seven

Suppression of Struan

The idea of closing down Struan church arose in 1818. This was proposed by the minister, the Reverend John Stewart, actively supported by John, the 4th Duke of Atholl, partly because both Struan and St Brides churches were in a "ruinous state".

John Stewart was born in 1781, the son of James Stewart, tacksman of Stank near Callander and Rebecca Buchanan. He was proposed for the parish by the 4th duke and ordained there in 1806. He was unanimously elected moderator of the Dunkeld Presbytery on 31 October 1820. He had four daughters and five sons, one of whom was Atholl Stuart who later became the first Free Church minister in Blair Atholl. He wrote the New Statistical Account of the parish in 1838 and died in 1843.[1]

The main argument of the duke and the minister was that in having just one church to serve the whole parish, it would "promote the object of a parochial establishment and the religious edification of the people better than two places of worship".[2] They therefore petitioned the Dunkeld Presbytery on 28 September 1819:

> In the Parish of Blair Athole there are two churches, one at Blair and another at Struan, being four miles distant, both in a ruinous condition; that publick worship is performed in English and Gaelic at Blair for two successive Sundays, and upon the third Sunday at Struan in Gaelic only, and as eight-tenths of the population of the Parish are within five miles of Blair, may it please the Reverend Presbytery of Dunkeld to take such steps as are necessary to find that the present churches of Blair Athole and Struan are unsuitable places for publick worship, and to ordain a new Church be built at Blair fit for the accommodation of the whole Parishioners in which publick worship shall be regularly performed every Lord's Day and by which the Religious Interests of the people will be promoted.[3]

It was rumoured around the district that the duke's real aim was to have "a splendid church built at his own gate of Blair for the purpose of adding some splendour to the approach to the Castle".[4]

Tradesmen Summoned
Presbytery responded favourably to this approach and agreed to hold a meeting the following month, on 14 October, to examine the state of the two churches. The minister was instructed to have masons and wrights available to give reports. He was also asked to make intimations about the forthcoming meeting from the pulpit. At this meeting, Alex Robertson, mason in Blair Atholl and John Christie, wright at the castle were asked under oath "to give a true and faithful verdict" to these questions:

1. What are the dimensions of each?
2. What is the state of walls and roof of each?
3. Do either of the churches admitt of being repaired so as to afford comfortable accommodation for the parishioners of both parishes who may be expected in ordinary circumstances to attend?[5]

Members of Dunkeld Presbytery and the parish heritors then visited the two churches, when both were "voluntarily condemned to the utmost extent". Rather than return to Blair Atholl church, the meeting adjourned to the inn because a doctor present declared that "it was unsafe to continue longer in the church of Blair". He continued, "It is from two to three hundred years old, and when the rest of the building is so ruinous, no one can seriously entertain such an idea."[6] Both churches were so far gone that presbytery had no hesitation in condemning them.

The tradesmen were then called upon to give their verdict on the fabric of the two churches:

> . . . we examined the church of Struan and found the walls and roof of said church in a quite ruinous state, incapable of repair. The length is seventy two feet and the breadth seventeen feet, inside measure, the height of the wall nine feet.
>
> We have in like manner examined the church of Blair, and find the walls thereof in a quite sufficient state as they stand, but the roof is entirely gone. The length of said church is 59 feet 6 inches and breadth 16 feet 9 inches within the walls, the height is 18 feet.[7]

Presbytery asked for a report on the third question: "whether the same be capable of being repaired so as to contain 650 people at the rate of 18 inches to each for bottom room" and the tradesmen's reply was: ". . . it is absolutely impossible to repair the Church of Blair so as to contain the number of people stated".[8] It was indicated moreover, that if Blair church were repaired, it would seat only about 300, less than half the number of communicants at the last count. The minister explained that: "In summer I preach in the open air and if not, the doors crowd with people who have no seats in the church".[9]

Robertson Opposition

At this point in the proceedings a paper was submitted to presbytery by heritors, mainly from Glen Errochty, among whom were: Colonel Alexander Robertson of Struan, the clan chief; Alexander Reid of Blairfettie and his factor, the Reverend John Robertson; Duncan Robertson of Auchleeks and Dr Alexander Robertson of Alexandria, his trustee; Patrick Robertson of Trinafour, Lieutenant in the Royal Marines; James Robertson of Kindrochet; Lieutenant General William Robertson of Lude; Patrick Robertson of Toldunie and the Four Merk Land of Lude.[10]

They objected strongly to one church being built in Blair with no worship at Struan, as this was, "highly inexpedient and adverse to the interests of religion among the people with whom they are connected . . ." and for the following reasons:

1. The suppression of Kirks does not rest with presbytery but is the responsibility of the Lords of Council and Session as commissioners for churches. This was based on the 30th Act of the second session of the first Parliament of William and Mary in the year 1690 which gave power as quoted:

... to the Lords and others of the commission thereby appointed for plantations of kirks and valuations of teinds, to disjoin too large and spacious parishes, to cause, erect and build new churches and to annex and dismember parishes as they think fit.[11]

2. While they admitted that the present churches "are in a ruinous state, and even disgraceful to the country, as places for publick worship and have long been so", they were agreeable to contribute to building two new churches.
3. If there was to be only one church, Blair Atholl was by no means the central point in the parish which is around 30 miles in length. They maintained that it should be at Struan because "it is undeniable that a much greater part of the inhabitants live nearer to the present kirk of Struan . . .".
4. Proof that Blair was not regarded as the centre was demonstrated in 1750 when the manse and glebe were removed two miles to the west, to Baluain, about midway between the two churches.
5. The heritors believed that the application to suppress Struan must have arisen "from some mistaken notion . . . which it is the duty and will of the Presbytery to prevent by guarding the religious Rights and privileges of the whole inhabitants without any paltry consideration of expence. . . ."[12]

The Robertson heritors concluded by asking presbytery to dismiss the application:

... as incompetent in so far as respects the suppression of the parish church of Strowan and to find that there must be two new Parish Churches built, or, if a central situation can be fixed upon, which will accommodate the whole inhabitants . . . and also to secure and enclose in a sufficient manner the burial grounds. . . .[13]

There were two reasons why the Robertson heritors were so vehement in their opposition. Firstly they had a very strong association with the church where the clan chiefs and many of their own ancestors had been buried for centuries. Secondly there was the question of distance of up to twelve miles from the church at Blair Atholl for many of the tenants and cottars in this part of the parish.

Presbytery Response
Presbytery, "taking every circumstance into consideration, after the most careful investigation and inquiry" decided that Blair church should be rebuilt to accommodate 650 people, including room for communion tables. With regard to Struan, they did not find it expedient to rebuild it and were to leave this matter until after Blair had been enlarged. The minister was instructed to preach there occasionally "if he can with safety to himself and the Parishioners".

The Errochty heritors were appalled at this verdict and protested vigorously, appealing to the Synod of Perth and Stirling. This appeal was rejected by the presbytery who considered it was "an incompetent court" but would allow it to be heard by the Court of Teinds. The synod met in October 1818 and concurred with presbytery, saying it was not in their remit to investigate the civil question of building new churches" and refused to entertain this part of the question". However, that body had no hesitation in declaring that "religious worship be performed in Blair Athole and Strowan as formerly".

Population

A key element in the decision to rebuild Blair church was the distribution of the population in the parish, which in the 1820s was as follows:[14]

Residing upwards of 5½ miles west of Blair
who must pass the Church of Struan going to Blair: Totals

Glengarry excluding Woodshiel	179	
Glen Errochty including Woodshiel	257	
Bohespic	188	
Strathtummel and Port an Eilean	236	
Borenich, part of Bonskied	108	
		968

Residing from 2-4½ miles west of Blair and nearer to Struan than Blair:

Left bank of the Garry from the Manse to Calvine	261	
Right bank of the Garry from Clachan to Easter Invervack including Kindrochet	252	
Village of Carrick in Fincastle	25	
		538
Total population nearer to Struan than Blair		1,506
Residing ½ mile west of Blair and nearer to Blair than Struan with Woodend of Urrat		40
Total west of Blair		1,546

Residing east of Blair and including Blair Atholl House (Blair Castle):

Right bank of the Tilt including Blair from Dalness to Haugh of Blair	165	
Left bank of Tilt to the Fender, exclusive of the Four Merk Land of Lude	132	
Strathgarry, Clunes and the property of the Duke of Athol	132	
		429
Estate of Lude including the Four Merk Land of Lude	421	
Tenandry and Rienakyllich	102	
Estate of Coillebrochain	6	
		529
Total east of Blair		958
Total population of the united parish		2,504

The minister disputed these figures, maintaining that 1,158 people lived to the east of Blair and although he conceded that over a third of the population were part of the old Struan parish, he neglected to mention that of those living in the east of the parish, nearly a half belonged to the episcopal church at Kilmaveonaig.[15]

Robertson Dismay

The anger and dismay of the Robertson heritors is illustrated in their correspondence of the time:

Alexander Robertson of Struan to the duke:

11 October 1819

... I thought one church might be sufficient for the inhabitants of both parishes provided it was placed in any convenient situation. . . . Building the new church at Blair would by no means answer the purpose. This does not by any means, reconcile me to that reasoning which I shall most certainly resist as far as lays in my power.[16]

James Robertson of Kindrochet to his son, Captain Duncan Robertson:

23 December 1819
. . . I find you have heard something of the ungracious attempt made by the <u>Dictator of Atholl</u>, aided by his humble servants, the Presbytery of Dunkeld to do away with the Auld Kirk of Strowan. I presume you know His Grace is now become proprietor of that pendicle on which the Church of Strowan stands and it would appear he wishes to exert his Overwhelming Authority to make a clean sweep of everything that was formerly held sacred by the clan of Robertson. . . . Our worthy minister, I presume by the advice and with the consent of His Grace, presented a petition to the Presbytery of Dunkeld, every man of which, I am informed, owes his living to the Duke.[17]

Reverend John Robertson, acting for Blairfettie, to F. Graham, the Atholl factor:

30 October 1820
Mr Reid [proprietor] considers it his bounden duty . . . to attend as much in his power to the spiritual interest of his tenants, who live between eight and more miles from the church of Blair and therefore declines to give his sanction to any application to the Presbytery for the suppression of public worship at Strowan.[18]

James Robertson of Kindrochet to the duke:

5 November 1820
I am astonished at the erroneous information that the statement contained particularly with regard to the population and the distance at which the great portion of it is stated to reside in Blair. The result of the investigation is that your Grace has doubled the number of people living on your own estate west of Blair to what are on your Grace's property to the east.[19]

Robert Robertson of Auchleeks to the Reverend John Stewart:

8 October 1823
I cannot come to any other conclusion than that Strowan Church ought to be rebuilt. That the church needs rebuilding, none dispute. In its present state it is a disgrace to a Christian community.[20]

Robert Robertson of Auchleeks to H. Graham, lawyer:

11 October 1823
It appears to be quite clear that the suppression of the church of Struan could be a great evil to the parish. . . . But I beg leave to observe to you upon the impolicy of agitating the measure of pulling down or suppressing a church in these church building times. It will not fail to strike you how much it is the taste of the lower orders in the present day to rail at, attack and try to pull

down the higher. Neither would it have escaped your observation how readily, and how powerfully they are assisted in doing so by those who do not belong to their class.[21]

Some remained neutral, like Miss Ann Stewart, and her sister, of Bohally, who declined to become involved in the suppression of Struan.[22] The Robertson heritors were dealt a serious blow when one of their major supporters, General Robertson of Lude, died on 31 January 1820, after which the estate was run by trustees under James Scott. The duke had been told that if he informed the trustees of his plan for the two churches, he would probably procure their agreement to the proposed suppression. Robertson of Auchleeks had indicated that if this happened, it would be likely that other heritors would be advised to drop their opposition.

> James Scott, Lude Trustees, to H. Graham, lawyer:
> 11 October 1820
> It would be more advisable that the inhabitants should be provided with a place where they could hear Worship every Sunday than only once in three weeks. My only objection is the increased distance which however I do not think much of.[23]

He wrote again on 17 October:

> I hereby express my willingness as trustee on the estate of Lude to appear as a consenter to that measure, but not as an applicant. I give this consent on the understanding that the estate is to be put to no part of the expence of the proceedings.[24]

When the trustees realised that the proposal to suppress Struan was likely to result in a long and expensive lawsuit, they insisted that the duke relieve them of their share of the expenses incurred for any proceedings. "Unless I hear from you within eight days with the guarantee," James Scott wrote, "I will be withdrawing my consent."[25]

Within a year of the start of the presbytery proceedings, Toldunie had changed ownership and now belonged to the Hon. Peter Robertson, whose factor wrote to Humphrey Graham with his views:

> 21 October 1820
> I consider the plan you have prepared to be good for the heretors and parishioners by the suppression of Struan church and to have one only, more large and convenient near to the great bulk of the parishioners and I give my consent to it.[26]

The duke was keen to win round the Struan heritors and therefore wrote to Captain Alexander Robertson of Struan giving him the opinion of his legal counsel:

> . . . there is no reason to suppose that Strowan church would have been retained more than the churches at Lude and Kilmaveonaig. On the contrary, it seems obvious that as all the whole four were put under the charge of one clergy man, Strowan would have been suppressed entirely and the whole parishioners brought together in one church, viz. the Ecclesia Matrix at Blair which is the

centre of the population of the four parishes – where alone the sacraments have always been administered, where the parish school and post office are situated and the Poors Account kept.

When the whole parish was annexed there was no legal obligation to uphold the church of Strowan more than Lude and Kilmaveonaig and the motives of expediency which included them to do so has now long ceased.[27]

Heritors for the Suppression

Some heritors agreed to the idea of suppression, with Dr Alexander Stewart of Bonskeid insisting there was "an absolute necessity of building a new church at Blair Athole for the accommodation of the parish". Peter Robertson, factor of the Urrard estate told George Condie (the duke's Perth lawyer) that he was "satisified at the propriety, expediency and utility of one parish church at Blair that I concur in any proceeding. It is hard that the people of Struan should have preaching but one in every three weeks when they can hear it every Sunday." [28] Humphrey Graham met the Moderator of the General Assembly of the Church of Scotland, a man "completely conversant with church law" on 7 October 1820, writing afterwards to the duke that he "had expressed his opinion decidedly in favour of the suppression".[29]

The minister, as instigator of the suppression, had much to say about the potential benefits and advantages of it, as shown in the following observations:

23 October 1818
It is ridiculous to speak of the distance of Blair as throwing out the pale of the Church a people who have hitherto had but ⅓ share of that public religious instruction which they may now enjoy. . . .[30]

1820 Report
It is doubtful if Strowan has been acknowledged as a parochial establishment ever since the annexation of the four parishes; but merely considered as a Preaching House or Outpost of the parish. It has no district precentor, clerk or schoolmaster.[31]

30 November 1820
It would certainly be expedient to rebuild the church of Strowan if it be the object of the Presbytery to promote the interests of the Chapel of Kilmaveonaig. When there is a sermon at Strowan some of the people to the east of Blair will no doubt attend the Chapel of Kilmaveonaig rather than spend the Lord's Day in idleness: And it requires not great judgement to infer that it may be convenient to have a sermon at Kilmaveonaig when the parish minister is at Strowan. Kilmaveonaig would then become the rendezvous of dissenters of all descriptions.[32]

Feelings on the matter became acrimonious throughout the parish, especially between the Robertson heritors and the minister, who commented that:

In these days when the wildness of enthusiasm and the blasphemies of infidelity are abroad, it is much to be regretted that one of the representers and a commissioner for another heretor should wish to deprive the people of their estate, amounting to 350 souls, of one third of the yearly Sabbath. It is more than lamented that another of the representers, Colonel Robertson of Strowan should wish to restrict his tenants, half of whom are within two miles of Blair to the performance of a third part only of that public service. . . . And a third Representer Mr Robertson of Kindrochit, whose property is 3½ miles from Blair and upon which he and his family reside, shews by his present opposition that he and his people wish instead of keeping one day in seven holy unto the Lord, to hear his sacred word preached only once in three weeks.[33]

In September 1820 Humphrey Graham implied to the duke that those heritors against the suppression would perhaps not have opposed it at all and at least not gone to the lengths of contesting it in a court of law, had he kept them fully informed of his plans and the reasons and advantages for them.[34]

The Robertson heritors had also indicated that they would be satisfied if a new church, capable of holding the entire parish, was put up in a central situation and suggested West Cult (Cult Beg), which is a mile and a half west of Blair Castle. It appears in a crown charter dated 12 February 1504 in favour of Sir John Stewart of Balvenie, first Earl of Atholl, covering the settlements near the castle, including "Litilquylt". Until these settlements were cleared in the 1730s for landscaping purposes, Cult Beg was a one merkland.

By 1820 it was planned to make a new line of road from Craggan, east of Blair Atholl, across the River Tilt, by the side of the River Garry, which would reduce three miles of a "very bad road" to two miles of good road and would pass beside West Cult. These road-building plans were temporarily abandoned but it is still difficult to see any advantages of the new location. The minister explained there were no houses near it and only one or two families living between it and Blair Castle. The inconvenience for people living in the west and travelling to St Brides was more than balanced by the "comforts, accommodation and stabling which the village and inn of Blair Atholl affords".[35]

St Brides church in 1861 with the roof on the west side still intact.

The presbytery clerk maintained that to consider any other location was absurd, especially in a parish "where there are districts of fifty or sixty thousand acres inhabited exclusively by the Wild Deer of the Forest".[36] The minister insisted that moving the church to the west was removing it from the main area of population and in stormy weather, "could hardly expect a single hearer beyond his own tenants" (in Baluain).

The arguments became faster and more furious, with the minister himself contributing: "If a new church is necessary", he wrote, with the snide remark: "Why not retain or rebuild the Church of Lude (the walls of which are still standing) which is 4 miles north east from Blair." The duke's counsel was of a similar opinion, stating: "As the walls of the old church of the parish of Lude are still standing, the heritors might as well be called upon to rebuild it, as the ruinous church of Strowan."[37]

Heritors' valued rents were then assessed and divided between those assenting and opposing:[38]

		£ Scots
	Rent of Blair	3,119. 9. 7
	Rent of Struan	1,225. 5. 5
	Total Rent of the Parish	£4,344.15. 0

Heritors Assenting		Heritors Opposing	
	£ Scots		£ Scots
Duke of Atholl	2,817. 9.11	Robertson of Lude/Toldunie	650.10. 2
Urrard	197.13. 4	Robertson of Struan	270. 0. 0
Bonskeid	120. 0. 0	Blairfettie	80. 0. 0
Port an Eilean	21. 9. 7	Auchleeks	80. 0. 0
Fincastle	7. 3. 3	Trinafour	64. 8. 9
		Kindrochet	36. 0. 0
	£3,163.16. 1		£1,180.18.11

Total Rental of duke's estate in Old Blair Parish	£2,122.13. 3
Total Rental of duke's estate in Old Struan parish	£694.16. 8

The duke also produced a profile for each of the Robertson heritors and was aware that General Robertson of Lude's motives for his "opposition were well known". He maintained that Robertson of Struan and Reid of Blairfettie, who lived some way distant, knew very little about the church, not having been in it for at least twenty years. It was observed too, after the general's death, that the Lude Trustees' decision to consent to the suppression considerably weakened the Robertson case, reducing their rental value total by over fifty per cent, resulting in their financial power dwindling to about twelve per cent of the total rentals. Their combined rental value of about £500 was deemed by the duke to be – "too insignificant to entitle them to much consideration in forming parochial arrangements when the total rent of the parish is £4,344".[39]

Lords of Council and Session

The heritors opposing the suppression of Struan appealed to the Lords of Council and Session, the highest church court in Scotland. They came to the conclusion that the decision to build a new church was not on account of the state of St Brides but rather that it was too small to hold the whole parish. ". . . our said Lords Justice can never tolerate a proceeding of that kind", they observed and continued:

These are not the times for suppressing churches, when Government are doing everything in their power to find the means of increasing their numbers; nor is it fit, or even decent, that a population of 1,000 persons at least should be left altogether without the benefit of religious instruction or deprived of the very scanty means this parish of Strowan has had in times past. . . . [40]

Their Lordships also observed that if only one church was to be rebuilt:

. . . certainly the most commodious for the great body of the united parishes is that of Strowan. . . . It is the great body of the inhabitants who are really interested in this question, certainly more so than the Duke of Athole.

Their final decision was that the church of Struan could not be closed "and the building of both parish churches at Blair Athole and Strowan should proceed at the same time. . . ." [41]

St Brides Rebuilt
Within a few months of this decision, St Brides was re-roofed and opened again for worship. However, matters changed in 1822, when the old military road through Kilmaveonaig and Blair, north of the castle, was closed and a new route was opened through the Haugh of Blair, with the completion of a new bridge across the River Tilt.

Presbytery met on 18 September 1823 to inspect a site for a new church on the Haugh of Blair, which it had agreed would be more convenient for heritors and parishioners, particularly as access to St Brides was difficult. The duke had indicated that he was willing to "give, sell and assign an acre of ground if required, and that forever". The church, including communion tables, was to be capable of holding 650 people. [42]

With all the heritors' thoughts and energies being directed towards the new Blair Atholl church, no improvements were undertaken at Struan. The Robertsons favoured a new church be built on the site of the old one, capable of holding a congregation of 600. They offered to donate the site for the church and churchyard and an acre and a half for a manse and garden. They also offered, at a moderate rent, to provide four to five acres to allow a minister to keep a horse and a cow. [43]

Throughout 1824 opposition by the minister to a new church at Struan continued, as is revealed in a letter from Robert Robertson of Auchleeks to the duke:

7 April 1824
Mr Stewart is strongly opposed to having a church in that situation at all and for the following reasons:
First, that if Struan church be rebuilt he apprehends some part of his congregation may be drawn away from him.
Secondly, if rebuilt he would have a duty to perform in two churches instead of one. [44]

Auchleeks complained again to the duke later that year:

23 October 1824
The Minister is decidedly hostile to plans to rebuild Strowan. Clergymen should not be allowed a voice in it [suppression]. If churches were suppressed

then a clergyman gets rid of his entire duty. He has no right to interfere in this question and the more specially when such influence is a direct opposition to the wishes of the inhabitants.[45]

A petition signed by the heads of households, totalling over 1,500 people living in the western and more distant parts of the parish was drawn up, and read as follows:

29 July 1824
Strowan Church is five miles from Blair and five miles from the greater part and nearly ten miles from the western and more remote parts of its district. Parishioners complain of being almost shut out from the comfort of religious instruction by reason of the infrequency of public worship, the service being performed only once in three weeks. Pay a clergyman to officiate twice on Sunday, once in Gaelic and once in English. Strowan should be rebuilt on the old ruin, preserving what will always be very dear to them, the stance of their ancient altar and the graves of their kindred and friends.[46]

Finally, on 29 March 1825, victory for the Robertson heritors was achieved, when Dunkeld Presbytery announced that they "are of opinion that an Erection at Struan, or somewhere in that neighbourhood is highly expedient".[47]

References

1. *Fasti*, Scott
2. BCCR Bundle 1228
3. SRO CH 2 106/13
4. BCCR Trunk 33 XVIII
5. Ibid
6. Ibid
7. SRO CH 2 106/13
8. Ibid
9. BCCR Trunk 33 XVIII
10. SRO CH 2 106/13
11. BCCR Trunk 33 XVIII
12. SRO CH 2 106/13
13. Ibid
14. BCCR Trunk 33 XVIII
15. BCCR Bundle 1227
16. BCCR Trunk 68 (9) 277
17. J I R
18. BCCR Trunk 33 XVIII
19. BCCR Bundle 1227
20. Ibid
21. BCCR Trunk 68 (12) 316
22. BCCR Trunk 33 XVIII
23. BCCR Bundle 1227
24. BCCR Trunk 33 XVIII
25. Ibid
26. Ibid
27. Ibid
28. Ibid
29. BCCR Trunk 68 (10) 379
30. BCCR Bundle 1227
31. BCCR Trunk 33 XVIII
32. BCCR Bundle 1228
33. BCCR Trunk 33 XVIII
34. BCCR Trunk 68 (10) 370
35. BCCR Trunk 33 XVIII
36. Ibid
37. Ibid
38. Ibid
39. Ibid
40. Ibid
41. Ibid
42. SRO CH 2 106 /13
43. BCCR Trunk 33 XVIII
44. BCCR Bundle 1227
45. Ibid
46. Ibid
47. SRO CH 2 106/14

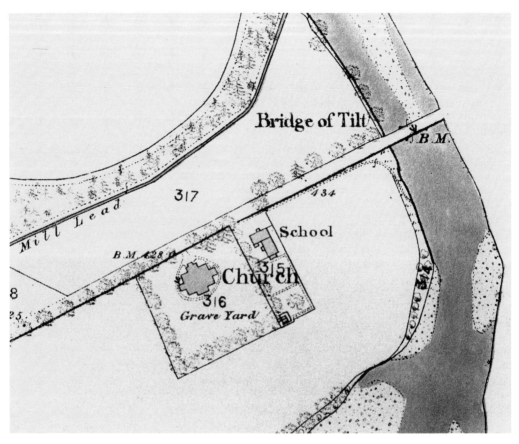

Extract from the Ordnance Survey First Edition 25 inch map showing Blair Atholl church.

eight

Blair Atholl Church

At a heritors' meeting held on 17 March 1824, six estimates for building a new church at Blair Atholl were considered:

1. John Stewart and Andrew Stevenson – £1,255, allowing £35 for materials from the old church.
2. A McKenzie, Peter Logan and James Reid – £1,060
3. John Angus – £1,039, allowing £45 . . .
4. Charles Sim – £1,060
5. Alex Robertson – £1,045, allowing £45 . . .
6. James McArthur – £1,145, allowing £20 . . .

The meeting approved the acceptance of the lowest estimate, so the contract was awarded to John Angus, a Dunkeld builder, for his tender of £994.[1] The builder was told that the vault in St Brides could not be touched, nor the duke's pew and the entrance to it, on account of the stonework, "which has been taken considerable pains with". He was also instructed not to touch the bell tower as the duke had "expressed an intention of reserving the tower".[2] Later, the builder reported that because of these restrictions, he had suffered a considerable loss and the heritors agreed to give him an allowance of £10 in recompense.

The new church was to seat nearly 600 people, with a gallery on the east and west ends. The contract between the heritors and the builder was as follows:

> . . . Whereas the said Heritors have resolved to build a new church in the Haugh of Blair between the new bridge of Tilt and the mill road on a spot to be pointed out by Frederick Graham Esq., factor to His Grace the Duke of Atholl, conforming to a plan and elevation designed and drawn up by the late Archibald Elliot Esq., Architect in Edinburgh. . . .
>
> The said John Angus binds and obliges himself to erect build and finish the said church in a good sufficient and workmanlike manner and to provide all stones, timber, lath, nails, locks, keys, lead, iron, sand, lime and all other materials. The church to be completely finished by and delivery of keys to the said minister on 1st June 1825. Said John Angus binds and obliges himself to maintain said church wind and watertight in the walls and roofs for the space of two years.[3]

Builder's Specification
Specifications were laid down for every part of the building:[4]

Digging and Foundation
  Foundations of the walls not to be laid at less than one foot under the

lowest part of the surrounding ground and more if necessary to obtain a proper foundation and the doors at the east and west ends of the church were to be at least nine inches above the high part of the ground. . . .

The foundations to be laid 3 feet 6 inches broad with large flat stones nine inches thick and the walls then to be set off at 2 feet 6 inches thick. . . .

Building Work

The walls to be good rubble work solidly built with stone and lime regularly banded hard packed and grouted with lime, the lime to be mixed with a due proportion of clean sharp sand – Bone timbers to be built in all the walls inside the church. Duke's seat and session house not to exceed two feet apart. . . .

Hewn Work

All the windows and doors to have freestone sills lintles and rybets all laid on their natural beds. . . . The steps up to the porch to be droved freestone – the two hanging stairs leading to the galleries to be freestone neatly jointed and droved on both sides. The two staircases, the porch, the passages in the middle of the church, the opening in front of the pulpit and under the same to be laid with whinstone pavements. The session house and miniser's room to have freestone jambs and hearths – an elliptic pointed arch to be thrown over the opening at the Duke's seat. . . .

Joisting

The arch in Blair Atholl church above the recess that formerly housed the duke's private pew.

The gallery joists to be fixed at a wall pleat at the top and dovetailed into the beam below – the under head of the beam to be nine feet from the floor and each seat to rise seven inches above another and the backs to rise in proportion. . . .

Couples

The couples to be eight inches at the bottom, six inches and one half at the top, two and a half inches thick and placed sixteen inches apart. . . .

Tower

The tower to be joisted at the uppermost offset in the wall – to form the bell tower . . . and a hatchway to be in the floor of the bellhouse two feet six inches square, to have a flap hinged and neatly finished below and a ladder made to answer the same. . . . The bell to be hung on two beams nine inches deep, six inches thick, to have a twelve inches wall hold and properly bound together. The bell to be rung by a wheel of proper size.

Windows

The windows to be made with cases and two sashes to be two inches thick, glazed with second crown glass to receive one coat of white paint before they are glazed and another after it.

Doors

The doors of the church to be in two halves and those between the church and staircase to be hinged so as to fold close back to the wall; all the other doors to be whole. The outer doors to be flush panneled and beaded and the rest to be panneled and mouldings on both sides. . . . The stair to the minister's room to be one inch and an eighth thick sufficiently put up to have deal bannisters and a hand rail. The room and session house to have panneled shutters and finished with plain facings and skirtings. The wall press in the session house to have a bound door one and a fourth thick and three shelves. The stairs to the galleries to have cast iron bannisers and a strong elm or oak hand rail.

Seating

The seats to be altered so as to admit of fixed communion, tables to be along the centre of the church five feet wide and the passage on each side to be two feet nine inches clear. The passages at the end of the communion tables to be five feet wide and the length then to be divided into five equal parts. The middle seats to have a door in each side and the ends, one door each. The Duke's seat and porch to be eighteen inches higher than the church, the front the ends and the back to be panneled and the front to have a neat cornice and an architrave moulding round the arch. All the seats in the low church to have panneled doors, likewise the front seats of the galleries.

Pulpit

The floor of the pulpit to be five feet six inches above the floor of the church. All the pulpit and precentor's desk to be panneled and to have torus beads on the pannels – to have a neat cornice and the doors to have suitable hinges and locks. The canopy to be neatly made according to to a drawing to be made out while the work is going on. . . .

Lathing

All the walls of the building except the staircases to be lathed. All the ceilings to be lathed and two sounding holes left in the church. All the walls of both church and galleries to be lined with three fourth deals to the height of the top of the seats. . . .

Slating

The roofs to be perfectly slated with dark blue slates from Newtyle Quarry, put on with nine pound nails japanned with boiled lintseed oil. . . .

Plumber Work

The ridges to be covered with milled lead fourteen inches broad, to weigh five pounds per superficial foot. The roof of the tower to be covered with lead weighing seven pounds per superficial foot. The water to be discharged into four-inch pipes of seven pound lead.

Plaster Work

... The plaster to be done with good English lime mixed with a due proportion of sand and hair, or if the lime of the country is found to answer equally well it may be used.

Quality of Wood

The wood for the sleepers and ground floor to be larch. The pulpit, the front of the galleries and the Duke's seat to be foreign wood or very clean Wey-mouth pine. All the rest of the timber for completing the building to be good scotch fir.

The contract laid down a number of additional stipulations which had followed:

1. All timber, not foreign, must be purchased from the duke's plantations.
2. All foundations to be dug out and rubbish removed.
3. Wood for doors, windows, and other purposes will be prepared by June 1824.
4. Mason work must be ready for the roof by 1 October.
5. Roof to be completed by 1 November.
6. Plaster work to be completed by 1 April 1825.
7. Keys to be handed over on 1 June.

Payments were to be in stages as follows:

Blair Atholl church, built in 1825.

First	£250 when the foundations were laid.
Second	£300 when the roof was complete.
Third	£250 when the plaster work and gallery seating were finished
Fourth	£289 when work was completed and taken off the builder's hands.

Dividing the Cost

It was agreed that John Angus would be responsible for collecting payments from each heritor according to his "valued rents" which were arrived at as follows:[5]

Heritor	Valued Rents	Proportion by Each	No. of Bottom Rooms for Each	Percentage
	£ s d	£ s d		
Duke of Atholl	2,643 11 6	624 18 3	367¾	63
Lude	696 15 3	164 14 2	96¾	16
Strowan	270 13 4	63 19 7¾	37½	6
Tenandry	147 13 4	34 18 2	20½	4
Auchleeks	144 8 9	34 2 10¼	20¼	4
Bonskeid	120 0 0	28 7 4¼	16¼	3
Toldownie	62 15 3	14 16 8¾	8½	1½
Blairfittie	55 1 8	13 0 5¼	7½	1¼
Kindrochat	35 0 0	8 5 5¾	4½	¾
Portnallan	21 9 7	5 1 6¾	3	½
Half of Carrige	7 10 0	1 15 5½	1	___
	£4,204 18 8	£994 0 1¼	583½	100%

The Duke of Atholl had by far the largest share with his rents being 63 per cent of the total and therefore his contribution was £624.18.3d and with the allocation of 367 seats, this gave him 63 per cent of the seating space.

On 25 September 1825 the church was inspected by two independent witnesses, James McArthur, builder and John Christie, carpenter, who found "the whole to be completed in a proper and workmanlike manner and that the contractor had in all respects fulfilled his engagement."[6] The heritors met in the new church for the first time on 29 September and approved the work with the exception of removing rubbish and hanging the bell which had come from St Brides. Mr Robertson, carpenter, provided a new rope and five beams for his own scaffolding, necessary for access to the bell and his account came to £1.1.0. The bell was hung on 6 October and on the same day the keys were handed over to the minister.[7]

The bell, which is 17⅞ inches in diameter, was cast by John Meikle of Edinburgh and is a fine example of his work.[8] It hangs between two beams just below the roof of the tower and is inscribed:

FOR JOHN MARQUES OF ATHOL LORD PRIVIE SEAL AD 1688.

Allocation of Seats

The duke's Perth lawyer, George Condie, was authorised to contact the County Sheriff in order that seating arrangements should be divided "according to legal form". The duke, as Patron of the parish was entitled to first choice of a pew and the next best was also given to him as the largest heritor. Each heritor was allowed to choose a pew for himself and his family, according to the size of his valuation

1828 seating proposal for Blair Atholl church.

and this governed the number of seats he could claim for his tenants. The parish minister was entitled to a "commodious seat" for his family, usually adjacent to the pulpit and some seats were set aside for the poor.[9]

The sheriff had decided on the dividing up of the church by 5 February 1826. He allocated two of the three square pews in front of the duke's to Bonskeid and Port an Eilean, while the elders were given the large pew on the west side of the pulpit. Next to it was the pew for Blairfettie and Carrick. The minister's pew was beside the pulpit with Toldunie next to it. The remaining pews on the ground floor, twenty four at 153 inches each in length and eight at 72 inches each, were all allocated to the duke's tenants. The east gallery had ten pews, each about 200 inches long , nine of which were given to Lude and one to Tenandry. The west gallery again had ten pews, split between Robertson of Struan and Auchleeks, Tenandry and other Atholl estate tenants.[10]

Threat of Litigation

Allocation of seats sometimes gave rise to disputes, which in one recorded case even threatened legal action. Mrs Reid, a widow in Bridge of Tilt, and therefore a Lude tenant, received a letter in January 1891 from Tods, Murray & Jamieson, the duke's Edinburgh lawyers, over the occupancy of an Atholl estate pew. Mrs Reid had already been asked by John Robertson, the Atholl factor, to vacate the pew because "it was now required for the use of His Grace's tenants". According to the lawyers, the pew, near the pulpit, had been given to her late husband, William Reid, on account of his deafness. They maintained that the pew "unquestionably forms part of the sittings belonging to the Athole estate" and asked her to vacate it within seven days, failing which: ". . . we shall however reluctantly be compelled to take out an interdict against you and your family continuing to use it . . .".

William McInroy, the laird of Lude, was most indignant at the way one of his tenants was being treated and instructed Mrs Reid and her family to continue to occupy the pew. Within two days he had answered the lawyers' letter, starting by suggesting "in perusing such a remarkable document I am willing to believe that you are in ignorance of the facts of the case." He insisted that the duke had no legal right to dispossess anyone from their pew and that the letter contained a number of inaccuracies. William Reid had never been deaf and his present pew was substituted in 1871 when alterations had taken place and no fresh allocation of pews made. He forcefully pointed out that his tenant had been a regular sitter since before the duke had been born.

He went on to question the duke's need for another pew. "There are at least 100 sitters in the body of the church vacant on most Sundays", he observed. This excluded the area in the porch set aside for the duke's servants which accommodated 55 people "and on an average 6 or 8 constitutes the attendance there, often no more than 2 or 3! Might it not be as well to fill up these instead of indulging in petty persecution of my tenants", he urged.

He asked the duke to call a meeting of heritors and attend in person to state his case when: "In proving his right to the pew in question, and vacating those at present occupied by his tenants, which belong to other heritors, I will arrange for the Reids to sit elsewhere." [11] There is no evidence that this matter was pursued by the duke and presumably it was quietly dropped.

Ministers

John Stewart carried on his ministry in Blair Atholl as the first minister in the new church, continuing until his death in 1843. He was succeeded by the

Reverend Dr Alexander Robertson Irvine, born in Dunkeld on 30 January 1806, the son of Alexander Irvine, minister of Little Dunkeld. He was educated at the Royal School of Dunkeld and the universities of St Andrews and Edinburgh, before being ordained to Foss church in May 1830. From there he moved to Fortingall in 1842 and was then called to Blair Atholl where he began as minister there in August 1843.

He married firstly, Margaret, a daughter of Joseph Stewart Menzies of Foss in 1833 and they had one daughter. From his second wife, Sophia Jane, only daughter of Captain Duncan Robertson of Kindrochet, whom he married in 1844 he had five children. Their daughter Sophia married John Robertson, factor to the Duke of Atholl and their son Alexander later became minister of Clackmannan.

The Reverend Dr Alexander Irvine died in 1867 and the duke presented as his successor the Reverend Norman Macleod who came to Blair Atholl and Struan from St Columba's parish in Glasgow. He was called to St Stephen's parish in Edinburgh in 1875, when the vacancy was filled by the Reverend James Fraser in the following year. The son of Roderick Fraser who worked for the Inland Revenue, he was educated at Fort Augustus School, Inverness Academy and the universities of St Andrews and Edinburgh. He was ordained as minister of Tarbert in 1864, moved to Dingwall in 1872 and four years later came to Blair Atholl, where he remained until 1908. He died on 1 September 1914 and is buried in Blair Atholl graveyard.

The next minister to come was the Reverend Donald Lamont, born in Tiree in 1874, son of John Lamont and Euphemia McFadyen. He was educated at Raining's School, Inverness and Edinburgh University. In 1902 he was ordained to Glen Urquhart church and transferred to Blair Atholl in 1908. During the First World War he was a chaplain to the troops at Gallipoli in 1915-16, an examiner in Celtic languages in Edinburgh University from 1903-1906 and editor of the Gaelic supplement in the Church of Scotland magazine *Life and Work*. He died in 1946 having served the parish for thirty eight years and his memorial in the churchyard reads:

The Reverend Donald Cameron, minister of Blair Atholl & Struan from 1947 to 1979. (Courtesy of Atholl Country Collection)

Reverend Donald Lamont 1908-1946
Himself a true man of God.
He showed to his people the things of God
through the wisdom of his preaching
and the excellence of his example.

He was succeeded by another Gaelic-speaking minister, the Reverend Donald Cameron, a native of Argyllshire, who was called to the parish in 1947, until he retired thirty two years later.[12] His successor in 1980 was the Reverend James Duncan, who retired in 1995, being followed by the Reverend Neil Gow, who was ordained to Blair Atholl, as his first charge, in March 1996.

Queen Victoria
Blair Atholl church's most eminent visitor, Queen Victoria, attended morning service there on Sunday 15 September 1844, accompanied by Prince Albert. The queen was staying at Blair

*Contemporary
sketch of Queen
Victoria and
Prince Albert
arriving for the
service in Blair
Atholl church in
1844 during their
stay in Blair
Castle.*

Castle for a three-week rest after the birth of her fourth child, Prince Alfred and she had insisted that regardless of the weather she would go to church on her first Sunday there. She asked Lady Glenlyon to sit beside her in the church to help her follow the presbyterian service. The duke's pew opposite the pulpit was specially lined with crimson satin, cushioned and carpeted for the occasion.

The minister, the Reverend Dr Alexander Irvine, was informed that the whole service should not last more than one and a half hours and that the queen was in the habit of listening to a sermon of no more than twenty five minutes. The queen, dressed in a black satinette gown and mantle, with a white bonnet, listened intently to the minister, whose text for the sermon came from St Matthew, Chapter 5, Verse 13: "Ye are the salt of the earth". It was agreed that "he gave a plain, lucid and earnest exposition of his subject and that Her Majesty could not have had a better illustration of the Presbyterian Worship, as it is celebrated today".

At the end of the service, the old practice in Highland parishes of collecting the offering from each member of the congregation was performed as usual with a long-handled ladle. After the service the queen emerged in pouring rain to a guard of honour of Atholl Highlanders lined up on each side of the entrance, who escorted her in her carriage back to Blair Castle.[13]

References

1. BCCR Bundle 1227
2. BCCR Trunk 68 (14) 77
3. BCCR Bundle 1227
4. Ibid
5. Ibid
6. Ibid
7. BCCR Trunk 69 (1) 346
8. PSAS Volume 122
9. BCCR Bundle 1285
10. BCCR Trunk 69 (2) 53
11. BCCR Bundle 1227
12. *Fasti*, Scott
13. *Glasgow Citizen* 27.9.1844

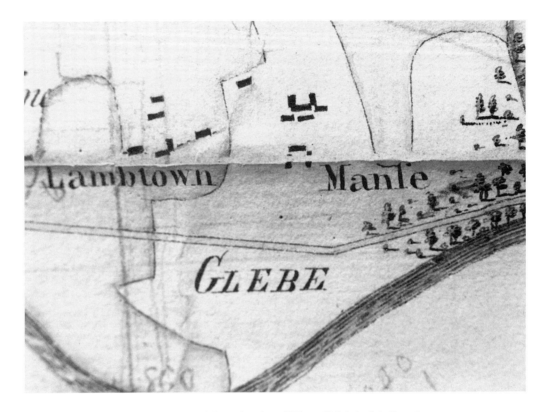

The minister's glebe, taken from "Plan of Blair in Atholl . . ."
by James Stobie, 1780.

nine

Blair Atholl Manses and Glebes

The right of a minister to a manse and glebe was passed by the Scottish parliament in 1563, in an act stipulating that "a reasonable and sufficient house should be built for them beside the church". In 1572 another act decreed that the extent of a glebe was to be at least four acres and again in 1606 another act laid down that where no arable ground was adjacent to the church, the minister should receive four soums for each of the four acres, from the best pasture near the church. A soum was a measurement of livestock headage on pasture and in Atholl it covered land that grazed ten sheep or one cow, although this varied according to height above sea level and quality of soil. Another act passed in 1612 ordained that: ". . . all ecclesiastical persons were to hold repair and maintain their houses and manses in such a condition as might serve for their residence . . .".[1]

From Duncan's *Parochial Law* we learn that an act in 1644 conferred on presbyteries the power to allocate glebes at every parish church but all this changed in 1649 when a new act provided that heritors should build a "competent manse for the minister, not exceeding £1,000 Scots". This was thought to be fair, because by this time heritors had secured the larger share of church property. In 1663 an act declared that every minister, except those in royal burghs, should have grass for a horse and two cows and "shall have fewel, foggage, feal and devots". If there was no suitable church land near the manse, then heritors were bound to pay £20 Scots each year to the minister.

In those times, when minister and parishioners alike, lived off home produce, a glebe was indispensable. Cattle were kept for the supply of milk, crops were cultivated and in the absence of good carriage roads, horses were essential for travelling round the parish. Manses, like churches, seemed to have been long and narrow and in the 17th century, like many other houses of the period, were built of stone and turf, with a thatched roof.[2]

St Brides Manse Rebuilt 1727

Up until 1750, the manse for St Brides was situated between the church and the old military road. In December 1727, Adam Brown, mason, appeared before presbytery and heritors to give an estimate for repairing it:[3]

		£ Scots
Item:	Building walls 3 feet higher and for 3 chimney heads	39.10. 0
Item:	Taking down the west gavel and rebuilding it with two vents	40. 0. 0
Item:	Building up the old door, stopping out a new one and making 4 windows	16. 0. 0
Item:	Taking down the middle gavel, putting two chimneys and enlarging the windows opposite the stair	25. 0. 0

		£ Scots
Item:	Building a brewhouse consisting of a rood and a half	27. 0. 0
Item:	Pinning and harling the manse inside and out	20. 0. 0
Item:	Winning windows, lintels, and chimney braces and skews for building walls	20. 0. 0
Item:	100 bolls of lime for the manse	66.13. 4
Item:	Winning stones and repairing the kail yard	5.13. 4
Mason Costs		£259.16. 8

Estimate of wright work from Patrick McInnes and John Lauder, excluding carriage, which heritors were to pay for: [4]

		£ Scots
Item:	Dales for flooring the garret in addition to the roof, making up the stairs and partitions, making up the old floor, sashes for windows, 5 doors for second floor and four doors for the first and the hall door amounting to 324 dales at 9 shillings Scots per piece	145.16. 0
Item:	Making two new cuples for the garret and supporting the stairs and partitions and window cases at £1 Scots per piece	40. 0. 0
Item:	Sarking the house, nailing the garret floor, fixing stair partitions, 6,000 double plenshions at £4 Scots per 1,000	24. 0. 0
Item:	1,200 single plenshions	3.12. 0
Item:	1,000 door nails	2. 0. 0
Item:	For locks and bands for nine doors	10.16. 0
Item:	Locks and bands for the principal door	3. 0. 0
Item:	Shutter bands, latches for windows	4. 8. 0
Wright Costs		£233.12. 0

John McCraw and Andrew McMillan submitted the Slaters' estimate: [5]

		£ Scots
Item:	3,000 skailie at £8 Scots per 1,000	24. 0. 0
Item:	Ground meal	6. 0. 0
Item:	8,500 nails at 6 shillings per hundred	25.10. 0
Item:	5½ roods at £10.10.0 per rood	55. 0. 0
Item:	For the roof	10.10. 0
Slater Costs		£121. 0. 0
Item :	Repairing the yard dyke	£5.13. 4

In February 1728 the minister, Robert Bisset learned that the heritors and the factor, Mr Murray, had decided that the old roof should be taken down and work begun on the repairs. When it was completed the manse was 48 feet in length, 16 feet wide with a slate roof and contained five rooms and office houses.

These estimates provide a wealth of material about the old manse beside St Brides, which was last inhabited two hundred and fifty years ago and has long since disappeared without trace. Up until 1727 it was probably a low-roofed, thatched building, which was heightened by three feet, another garret floor added and a brew house built. The contents of the tradesmen's estimates give an indication of the size of the house, its number of rooms, with their doors and windows.

The only pictorial record of this manse appears on John Tinney's and Charles Esplen's maps, both published in 1744. Their drawings clearly show three chimneys and five windows on the south side of the manse building sited slightly north-west of the church. James Dorret's map of 1758 has no trace of a manse at all but marks the addition of a row of cottages beside the road.

1742 Renovations
Within fifteen years further repairs to this manse were necessary and presbytery arranged for estimates to be put forward on 25 November 1742. John Sanders and James Robertson, Dunkeld masons, quoted as follows:[6]

		£ Scots
Item:	Taking down and rebuilding one rood and 2 ells of the forewall	26.13. 4
Item:	Enlarging one chimney, stopping another	15. 0. 0
Item:	36 bolls of lime for building	21.12. 0
Item:	Pinning and harling the house, inside and out and putting on skews and coping chimney heads	27. 0. 0
Item:	Winning stones and lime for harling the house, 24 bolls	18.18. 0
Mason Work		£109. 3. 4
Item:	Carriage of lime, stones and sand	£18. 0. 0

Estimate for wright work submitted by John Lauder and James Gentle:[7]

		£Scots
Item:	Laying garret floor and dividing the garret, 60 dales at 8d Ster. per dale	24. 0. 0
Item:	Lathing the manse and 68 dales	27. 4. 0
Item:	40 bolls of lime at 12 shillings per boll	24. 0. 0
Item:	12 stone of hair	6. 0. 0
Item:	8,000 door nails	9.12. 0
Item:	Carriage of timber, lime and hair	17. 4. 0
Item:	Workmanship, dividing garret, lathing and plastering the ceiling and walls on ground and first floors	81. 2. 0
Wright Costs		£189. 2. 0

Estimate for Slate Work submitted by Thomas Clark:[8]

		£ Scots
Item:	50 foot of rigan stone	10. 0. 0
Item:	Mending and pointing the roof and putting on rigan stones	6. 0. 0
Item:	900 single plenshions at 15d per 100	11. 3
Item:	Carriage of rigan stones	8. 8. 0
Slater Costs		£24.19. 3

Estimate of glass work for the manse submitted by Duncan Forbes, Tulliemet:

	£ Scots
Glass Work	£16. 5. 0

Manse and Glebe Exchange

St Brides glebe was located to the south of the manse and church, extending to within a few yards of the castle. By the late 1740s the 2nd duke had laid out policy parks, made lawns and paths and planted trees. This incorporation of the land round the castle resulted in a plan to relocate the manse and glebe. Not only would they be further away from the castle but be situated in a more central position between the two parish churches. John Stewart, the minister, commented on this in 1820:

> The manse and glebe from time immemorial was situated at Blair and the present house is the first manse that was built upon the lands of Balluaine. Its removal from Blair was owing to a cause which has often produced a similar effect in other parishes. The glebe was formerly in front and extended to within a few yards of Blair Castle, the residence of His Grace the Duke of Atholl. In order to acquire the glebe in property, which now forms a part of the lawn at Blair, His Grace gave the minister a very liberal exchange with a new manse upon the nearest adjoining land to His Grace's enclosures.[9]

Dunkeld Presbytery met on 23 November 1749 to discuss the exchange of manse and glebe. They inspected the three merk land of Easter Baluain, two miles west of Blair, which had been offered by the duke as a suitable location. Also present were "honest men" from the parish: Finlay Stewart and Duncan Moon, both from Baluain; Alexander Gow, Urrard Beg; Donald Frazer, Blair and John Robertson in Easter Balrobbie. They were asked to inspect the glebes of Blair and Baluain, judge the quantity and quality of both and give their verdict:

> . . . whether the three merk land with the biggings, grazings, shealings thereto belonging and the oak and birchwood growing on the said lands be in value equal to the present gleib of Blair, including twelve pounds Scots payed yearly by the Duke of Atholl to the minister for some parts and pertinents of the said gleib that some time ago was taken into his Grace's enclosure.[10]

After the five men had perambulated the marches of Baluain within the head-dykes, the presbytery asked them for their verdict, which was unanimous, in that the exchange was "fair and equal". Thomas Bissett of Glenalbert, Commissary and Thomas Bissett Junior, factors, informed them that the duke would "take the burden of those things upon himself and would build att Balluain a sufficient free manse and office houses and garden for the minister".[11]

1750 Inspection

The new manse was completed within a year and presbytery met there on 19 December 1750 to examine the work. They observed that "there is no garden and dykes for the minister according to the contract of excambion" and judged that "a garden 8 roods square with retaining dykes would be sufficient". They judged that the best location for this was north-west of the manse. George Moon, dyker in Blairuachdar, estimated the costs to build a dyke round it, 5 foot 3 inches high, supply stones and cover with "feal" would be £3 Sterling. The absence of "office houses" such as barn, byre and a brewhouse was noted and presbytery authorised the building of these as quickly as possible, instructing the minister to "maintain and uphold the present tennant houses in the said Town of Balluan or to demolish them upon his own charge".[12]

The following tradesmen were then called to give their verdicts on the standards of work that had been done in the new manse: James Gentle, wright in Dunkeld, who also undertook to report on the glazing and smith work; John Fisher, mason in Blair, who would also cover the plaster work: James Miller, slater. All were "solemnly sworn to give a true and faithful verdict with respect of the sufficiency of the manse".

Mason and Plaster Work—Both mason and plaster work were judged to be good and the measurements of the building were given as: length – 45 feet 8 inches overall; breadth – 20 feet 6 inches overall and height – 16 feet.

Slate Work—This was found to be "good and sufficiently done".

Wright, Glazing and Smith Work—This work and materials were "good and sufficient" although a few deals used for partitions was "blewwood". Measurements of the house within walls were, length – 40 feet, breadth – 15 feet 4 inches.[13]

Manse Interior

The manse was laid out as follows:

Laigh Floor—Kitchen 18 feet long and 15 feet 4 inches wide, having a vent and sash window with a wire frame on the outside. This included, at the back of the house, a Pantry, 11 feet 10 inches by 4 feet 2 inches with a wood-framed sash window and a Cellar measuring 7 feet by 6 feet. The second room on this floor was a Bed Chamber laid with deals, plastered ceiling and walls, a vent, and a sash window with a wire frame on the outside. There were two closets in it, one dark, the other with a timber framed sash window in the back of the house. This room was plastered on the stonework but not on the ceiling. Including the two closets, this room measured 17 feet 9 inches by 15 feet 4 inches. A wooden stair lighted by a sash window led up to the first floor.

First Floor—Here there was a Dining Room, 15 feet by 15 feet 4 inches, plastered on both walls and ceiling, with a vent, two sash windows and a shelved press lined with timber. The minister's Study was 12 feet 4 inches wide by 7 feet 1 inch deep, plastered on both walls and ceiling, with a vent and a sash window. A Bedroom measuring 15 feet 4 inches by 13 feet was also plastered on walls and ceiling, with a closet off it, also plastered and with a sash window.

All windows were glazed with crown glass and partitions were made from fir wood. Except for the stair window, all had shutters with bands and there was a double door with lock and stay band. All the rooms and closets had board doors with locks except for the garret which had a plain door with a lock. The principal rooms had an iron sneck on the doors and a locking cupboard.

Garret—A timber staircase, between the first-floor rooms, led to the garret floor, an open space, floored and beam-filled, with three glazed skylights and two gable lights.

It was agreed on account of the distance of this new manse from the church, that the minister should retain a room in the old manse in Blair or one in the new schoolhouse soon to be built, "to retire to on Sabbath and sermon days".[14] The Baluain manse was inhabited for only seventy years until it was replaced and now no trace of it or its outbuildings remain.

Glebe Boundary

On 25 September 1787, presbytery met to discuss the boundary of the Blair Atholl parish glebe at Baluain. James Stobie, land surveyor and Atholl factor, was present, along with "honest men" from the parish: John McGlashan, Blairuachdar; Alexander Gow and Alexander Stewart, Calbruar; Lachlan McIntosh, Balnacroft;

William Stewart, Dalchalloch; John Robertson, Wester Cultaloskin; Archibald McDiarmid, Easter Cultaloskin; Alexander Gow in Kirktown of Lude and John Stewart in Lambtown (Baluain).[15]

The boundary of the Blair Atholl glebe and arable ground belonging to the minister, James MacLagan, was submitted as being:

> The exclusive Right and Property of the grounds marked by us with march-stones placed in presence of the Presbytery, running northwards in a right line from the River Garry, by a stone placed near the side of the Garry, to a stone placed on a know near the middle of Wester Lambtown or Balluan, and from thence in a right line northward to a cairn placed on the side of a hill, forming the north west corner of the ground laid off; and from thence eastwards, by a line of cairns, to a rising ground from which the line runs by an angle eastward by a line of cairns to the dyke bounding Craigurrart Plantation, following said dyke southward to a corner at the top of a steep bank, from which it runs by a curved line of cairns till it joins the north west corner of the inclosure called Woodend, presently possessed by John Stewart, vintner at Blair Atholl and so joining the present marches of the glebe comprehending a part of the arable land of Wester Baluan or Lambtown, and hill within the lines above described, are a full equivalent value for all rights of Commonty formerly possessed by the minister of Blair Atholl on the adjoining grounds. And we further find that the whole materials of the Houses, Biggings, and Garden Dykes of the farm of Wester Balluan or Lambtown are the property of the Duke of Atholl.[16]

Presbytery agreed to the line of the boundary ". . . marked out with stones fixed and cairns raised at their sight . . .". They confirmed also that the duke was to pay for half the cost of building a new dyke on the west march, the Blair minister paying annually "in all time coming" five per cent of the cost of the other half. Both parties were to be responsible for maintenance and the new dyke was to be completed within eighteen months. The duke had also offered to build and keep in repair a dyke on the north and east lines of the march and until then, tenants in the glebe would enjoy the same privileges of common grazing as they had done before the enlarged glebe was agreed. The arable ground added to the glebe was to be exempt from the payment of mill multures and public burdens.[17]

Minister's Peat
In the 1797 agreement, the minister was given a right, with free access, to his peat moss in the hill above Pitagowan, as well as the right to collect turf and pull heather. Access was through a locked gate in the dyke built between his moss and the glebe, the key being handed over by the factor at the start of the peat cutting season in May and returned in August. This moss, on the shoulder of Creag Bhagailteach, was given to the minister in 1794, with tenants of Wester Baluain permitted to use it also. By 1809, the minister, John Stewart, was becoming alarmed at the number of tenants outside the glebe, who were using his moss: "This year not only those people but the people of Woodend and others [Calbruar and Balnacroft] have cast peats in that district of moss allotted for the glebe." Other tenants who had followed suit included a man from Tombane who had taken a "considerable quantity" while another from Struan "had gone to the same moss to make peats . . . If they are not prevented from going to our moss we will not have peats long as they are nearly run out already," he concluded.[18]

Shielings

James MacLagan's shieling was ten miles to the north in Glen Bruar, where there were problems caused by neighbouring tenants at the turn of the nineteenth century. Until a few years earlier, his shieling had covered most of the east side of Bruar Water but then a new shieling was made at Allt Cam A' Choire Mor, where the remains of six bothies are still visible. The minister's cattle grazed on the land occupied by the new shieling, and as he had to move them, he asked if his shieling, called Ruidh Dorcha Mhor, opposite Bruar Lodge, could be extended southwards. "My predecessor, [Alexander Stewart] excambed Ridorch-beg on the east side of the Bruir for half of Rie-dorch-more which I now possess", he wrote. The other half of his shieling was occupied by tenants of Easter, Middle and Wester Invervack (Stewartston) and in an effort to avoid trouble by ensuring that his shieling was not reduced in size, he asked for an enlargement. His letter to Thomas Palliser, the factor, concluded:

> You know that I am bound to the other heritors and to the presbytery not to suffer the minister of Blair to be deprived of his right. And so must be under the necessity of protesting against contrary proceedings. You know also how disagreeable and troublesome things of this kind must be to a man of 73, the age that is fond of peace and quiet.[19]

On the west bank of the Bruar Water, opposite Allt Sheicheachan, there is a boundary stone called the "Minister's March Stone" which marked the southern extremity of land rented by the Blair Atholl minister for shooting. It is half a mile south of Feith Mhinistier and although carrying no markings, was pointed out as such by the late Atholl head keeper, Alex McLeod then in the West Lodge.

Stipends

Ministers' stipends were fixed under the act of 1649. This permitted them to be augmented to eight chalders of victuals – a chalder being equivalent to 16 bolls,

The "Minister's March Stone" in Glen Bruar.

with a boll being a volumetric measure, equal to about 140 pounds [64kg]. When payment in kind could not be conveniently made, three chalders were given and money at a rate not exceeding £100 Scots per chalder, for the remaining five. £100 Scots was equal to £8.6.8 Sterling or £8.32 metric.[20]

The value of the Blair Atholl minister's stipend in 1794 was as follows:[21]

	£Sterling
Stipend as modified in 1753	52.10. 1
Augmentation of £5 and three chalders of victuals in 1794	63. 0. 0
	£115.10. 1

	£ Sterling	
Rent of Glebe of Kilmaveonaig	10. 0. 0	
Rent of Glebe of Lude	12.12. 0	
Rent of Glebe of Blair	60.10. 0	
Rent of Shieling of Blair	30. 0. 0	
		£113. 2. 0
Total Stipend		£228.12. 1

Glebes were, and today those still remaining, are let out to the highest rent that could be obtained. In October 1812, the minister, John Stewart, complained that it was eighteen years since the last increase and remarked that his stipend, exclusive of glebe rent, was the lowest in Scotland. He went on to say that:

As the expence of living has increased very much of late, the present incumbent hopes that an application to the Court of Tiends for a moderate augmentation of his stipend will not be deemed by His Grace the Duke of Atholl, either unreasonable or improper.[22]

Stewart was desperate to learn about any augmentation and after meeting the duke, wrote to him on 5 November saying ". . . it escaped me to ask how soon I might expect to be informed of the resolution . . .". Such was his anxiety that he travelled all the way to Dunkeld, only to find that "Your Grace was all that day in the country".

The following year the stipend was increased to six chalders of meal (oats) and barley and £630.4.7 Scots. £100 Scots was allowed to the minister for the purchase of communion elements. Stewart observed that: "The stipend is thus 96 bolls of victuals and £52.10.4 Sterling in money beside the allowance for communion". When the grain was converted to a cash equivalent, using the average price over the previous five years, the stipend totalled around £140 Sterling a year, while rent paid for the manse came to £14.12.0.[23]

By 1834, the rent from the glebes and shielings in addition to cash payments, was as follows:[24]

	£ Sterling
Kilmaveonaig	11. 0. 0
Lude	10.10. 0
Four Cottars	19. 0. 0
Wintering – about	10. 0. 0
Shieling rented by Lord Glenlyon (Ruidh Dorcha Mhor)	30. 0. 0
Part possessed by Minister	15. 0. 0
	£95.10. 0

Stewart never disputed that the glebes added considerably to his income but by the manse having been moved two miles in 1750, this "made private tuition an unavoidable expence in educating my children," he observed. "This affords but a small compensation for the additional laborious duties which is devolved in consequence of the union of the four parishes". [25]

When the glebes were revalued in 1823, the minister requested what was regarded as "an unreasonable priviledge" by Fred Graham, the Atholl factor, as he wished to have the right to set aside "the judgement of the jury which will be appointed for the valuation of the glebes". As the factor observed:

> Should their sentiment not coincide with his, which is most likely they will not, as he values the glebe of Baluain and Ruidorrochmore shealing at nearly £6,000 and the glebe east of Tilt at Kilmaveonaig at Lude at somewhere about £1,000 or more.[26]

Within about fifty years of being built, the manse was in need of repair and the kirk session arranged for it to be surveyed in 1806:

> . . . having inspected the manse and offices they find the same in a ruinous situation and want of considerable repair, and are of the opinion that Tradesmen should inspect the same so as to report and make out estimates of the expence to put them in complete and sufficient repair and also to give an estimate for rebuilding the manse in the front of the present offices and for converting the present manse into a part of the offices.[27]

Within a few weeks a price of £520 was tendered by John Stewart, a Perth architect but this was rejected. Another estimate was submitted by John Reid from Ballechin for repairing the manse only and his price of £280.1.0 was accepted. However, there is no evidence to show that these repairs were ever carried out. About the same time, the minister was complaining that his garden wall was in disrepair and proposed that it should be rebuilt at a cost of £15, which the session agreed to. In 1811 the minister told his heritors that his offices consisted of a barn, stable and byre and that two years previously he had built a peat house and cart shed, 51 feet long and 14½ feet wide, of stone and lime, with a slated roof. The cost of this was £38, excluding carriage and once again he asked to be reimbursed.[28]

New Manse
In 1823, following a meeting of heritors calling for temporary repairs at limited cost, tradesmen reported on the state of the manse. They recommended an immediate approach to presbytery stating the absolute necessity of building a new manse.[29] The heritors urged that this should be built, "in a situation most convenient for the parish which they, the heritors, are of the opinion ought to be near the new Bridge of Tilt . . . or contiguous to the new church as circumstances admit to for the convenience and comfort of the minister." [30] This idea was rejected and at a presbytery meeting on 18 September 1823, the heritors therefore agreed "to make specifications, to call for estimates, and to contract for the building in the situation of the present manse or near it".

Plans for a new manse were not drawn up until 1826. It was to cost about £600 and include material from the old manse. The minister insisted that new out-houses be built to the west of the existing building and turned down a suggestion that instead of repairing the present offices, the old manse could be

converted. The size of the manse proposed by the minister was 43 feet long, with seventeen rooms and windows, exclusive of two closets and a lobby and finished in a similar manner to Little Dunkeld manse.[31]

Estimates were obtained as follows:

	First Estimate	Second Estimate
Manse	£605	£670
Converting old manse into offices	£87	£82
Building new offices	£179	£184

A new estimate, based on a smaller manse was also obtained:

Manse	£579
Converting old manse into offices	£87
Building new offices	£179

Writing to the duke, the factor commented: "Your Grace will perhaps not approve of the plainness of the reduced plan and Mr Stewart will object to the reduced quantity of accommodation."[32] He also maintained that the offices were not worth repairing and there was little of any value except the slates, worth about £9.

In August 1826, the duke finally agreed to new offices being built immediately, as Mr Sim (the builder) had reduced his price to £150.17.0. He insisted that the new manse was delayed until 1827 or 1828 and that its outlay did not exceed £550. His fellow heritors decided, however, that although the estimate exceeded the stipulated amount by £28.19.11, "this was so trifling as not to warrant an interruption to the work". Building of the new manse began in 1827 and was completed by 4 June 1828, when it was taken off the builder's hands.[33] During an inspection by Dr Alexander Stewart of Bonskeid, he was of the opinion that everything had been well done "except for the kitchen and scullery, where the woodwork there has been rather hurried over".[34]

The Perth to Inverness railway line, which opened in 1863, passed right through the Blair Atholl glebe at Baluain so compensation was agreed, first with the Inverness and Perth Junction Railway and then with the Highland Railway Company. Payments to be made to the minister were as follows:[35]

1. Feu duty payable under decreet arbitral yearly at Whitsunday. £8.15. 3
   Interest on this sum is payable at the rate of 5 per cent
2. Annuity payable at Whitsunday yearly   £25. 0. 0
3. Expense of maintaining deer fence payable at Whitsunday yearly £1. 0. 0
                                                                  £34.15. 3

Bee Jock's Croft
The old settlement of Upper Baluain, now obliterated by modern plantations, lay half a mile from the manse. This became known as "Bee Jock's Croft", named after John Robertson, who lived there with his widowed mother in 1870, when he reclaimed the land and built a cottage. He paid a rent of £3 a year, "by special arrangement with the late Dr Irvine, minister of Blair Atholl, undisturbed by Dr Norman Macleod and myself [Reverend James Fraser] his successor in office".

John Robertson died in 1880, after which it was rented out to different tenants. By the end of the nineteenth century it was described as "that wretched house" by the minister, because it was virtually uninhabitable and the land value greatly reduced through lack of cultivation. It was described as a "common lodging house and private asylum" and the minister was keen to remove the tenants and pass the feu back to the duke. However, ". . . common humanity and Christian neighbourhood forbid my disturbing the Mackintoshes when poor Johnnie is dying," wrote the minister. "My idea is to leave them till November – there will be no eviction".[36]

References

1. DPD, Hunter
2. *New Spalding Club* 1897
3. SRO CH 2 106/5
4. Ibid
5. Ibid
6. SRO CH 2 106/6
7. Ibid
8. Ibid
9. BCCR Trunk 33 XVIII
10. SRO CH 2 106/7
11. Ibid
12. Ibid
13. Ibid
14. Ibid
15. SRO CH 2 106/10
16. Ibid
17. Ibid
18. BCCR Trunk 48 (10) 180
19. BCCR Trunk 48 (2) 77
20. *New Spalding Club* 1897
21. BCCR Bundle 1228
22. Ibid
23. Ibid
24. BCCR Bundle 1240
25. Ibid
26. BCCR Trunk 68 (13) 227
27. SRO CH 2 430/7
28. Ibid
29. BCCR Bundle 1227
30. SRO CH 2 106/13
31. BCCR Trunk 69 (2) 284
32. BCCR Trunk 69 (2) 185
33. BCCR Bundle 1226
34. BCCR Trunk 69 (4) 257
35. SRO CH 2 106/18
36. BCCR Bundle 224

Tenandry church, built in 1836 as a Chapel of Ease.

ten

Tenandry Church
Quoad Sacra

The 1st Duke of Atholl wrote to the moderator of the synod of Perth and Stirling in April 1710 suggesting that "Highland Parishes be more contiguous to their parish churches. . . . There can be nothing more obvious than that this will be an advantage both to the souls and bodies both of minds and people."

He observed how inconvenient it was to have parts of a parish ten or twelve miles distant from their church, when they lived within five miles of a church in another parish – "there was a plan layd down for this by a commission of the General Assembly ten or twelve years ago", he concluded.[1]

The Moderator of the General Assembly of the Church of Scotland, at that time, the Reverend Thomas Black, agreed with the duke's observations, ending a letter to him thus:

> May God abundantly reward your Grace's zeal for propogating the knowledge of Christ in these Highland Bounds, and may he pour the best of his Blessings upon your Grace's noble family.[2]

The synod of Angus and Mearns agreed with this idea also and wrote:

> 20 October 1721
>   . . . having a just sense of your Grace's concern to suppress immorality and to promote Religion and Virtue, are hereby incouraged to represent to Your Grace that the Northern parts of the paroches of Blair, Rattray, Bendochie and Alyth are through their great distances from churches, at a vast loss by want of Gospel Ordinance, whereby ignorance and vice do much prevail. Do therefore humbly intreat Your Grace would please to contribute your best endeavors for procuring a new erection in these bounds that thereby a gospel minister be got settled among them. . . .[3]

It was to be over a hundred years before a new church was built in the Atholl area. In 1834, Mr and Mrs James Hay of Seggieden, owners of Tenandry estate, approached the Scottish Society for the Propagation of Christian Knowledge (SSPCK) for help in building a church there. Mrs Christian Hay's reasons were: "To provide scripture instruction for a district otherwise destitute of the ordinary means of grace."[4] This applied particularly to the inhabitants living in the parish of Dull, north of the Tummel, who were cut off from their parish church not only through distance but with the added hazards of a loch and a fast-flowing river.

Chapel of Ease

The Hays, with their sister-in-law, Miss Mary Stewart of 55 Queen Street, Edinburgh, offered land that formed part of the eight pound land of Tenandry, as recorded in a sasine of 4 September 1832. With the land there was to be an endowment for building a "Chapel of Ease", the term used to describe churches located in places more convenient for people living at a considerable distance from their parish church.

Dunkeld Presbytery considered this offer on 10 February 1835, minuting the following:

> A Memorial was presented from Mr and Mrs Hay of Seggieden and a friend, praying leave to build and endow a Church for the accommodation of certain portions of the Parishes of Dull, Blair in Athole and Moulin. The Presbytery (in terms of the Act of Assembly 1798, in relation to Chapels of Ease) resolved that said Memorial could lie on their table till next meeting.[5]

Ordnance Survey map, second edition, 1900, showing Tenandry church and manse.

At the next meeting they agreed that the "said proposed erection will be highly conducive to the interests of Religion in that quarter". John Stewart, the Blair Atholl minister, was asked to inform his congregations from the pulpit, and the ministers from Dull and Moulin were invited to attend the following meeting on 28 April. At that meeting a draft of the proposed constitution for the Chapel of Ease was drawn up and submitted to the General Assembly.

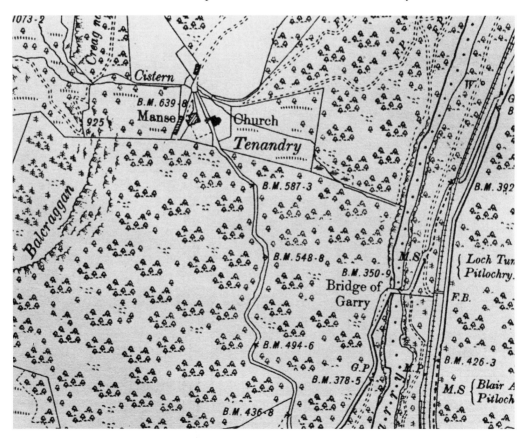

By June of that year the constitution for the Chapel of Ease had been approved:

1. The chapel shall be for the benefit of the inhabitants of the following places, First in the Parish of Dull: Glen Fincastle, Bonskeid House, Mains of Bonskeid, Shierglas and Pitdornie. Second in Moulin Parish: Urrard, Orchil, Old Faskally, Strathgarry. Third in Blair Atholl: Tenandry, Borenich, Coillebhrochain and Reinakyllich. This new district contained about 800 people. The chapel, containing about 400 sittings was vested in the three founders and on their deaths would pass to the SSPCK.

2. It would be used exclusively for the purpose of worship by a Minister of the Church of Scotland.

3. Its management was vested in the founders during their lifetime and then heritors and the kirk session.

4. No debts shall be incurred and the seats are to be free.

5. The managers and administrators will be under the control of Presbytery.

6. Minister's stipend shall not be less than £70 and more as funds allow.

7. The SSPCK in view of the lump sum they will be holding will pay the stipend at Whitsunday and Martinmas yearly.

8. Collections will be disbursed as follows: First; Payment of £8.6.8 for communion elements; Second: Payment of Precentor and officers; Third: Balance to be given to the heritors of the three kirk sessions in proportion to their numbers.

9. The founders shall nominate the first minister.

10. Where a vacancy occurs, the founders shall nominate a successor within six months. If there is a delay, Presbytery can nominate someone of their choice.

11. Every Sunday there will be a service in English and another in Gaelic and the sacrament of the Lord's Supper will be dispensed twice a year.

12. The founders will allocate seats for the minister, session and for proprietors of Tenandry, Urrard and Bonskeid and any others who contribute to the fund. The remaining seats are to be divided up among the inhabitants according to the population of each property, "always reserving ample space for the poor".

13. The precentor and officers shall be appointed by the Kirk Session.[6]

The founders provided an initial endowment of £1,500, later increased to £1,600 and agreed a stipend of £85 a year.

Tenandry Church Completed

The church, built to a simple "T" plan in a Tudor Gothic style, containing three galleries, was opened on 17 July 1836. The 14-inch bell, housed in a stone belfry, is inscribed: MACFARLANE & CO PERTH FOUNDERY [sic] 1835.[7]

There were 54 pews – 28 downstairs and 26 in the galleries, divided thus: Bonskeid 9½ pews; Fincastle 8; Tenandry 7; Urrard 6; Lord Glenlyon 5½; Shierglas 5; Old Faskally 4; Rienakyllich 3; Strathgarry 2; Poor 2; Session 1 and Minister 1.[8]

In addition to the proprietors named in the constitution, others had also made donations. The estate of Strathgarry was one, and was given pews 33 and 34, to be divided amongst its tenants. Mr Butter, proprietor of Old Faskally, by virtue of the population of his estate, was entitled to another pew so number 39 was transferred to him from Tenandry.[9]

In 1837 the population of the new parish was made up as follows:[10]

Galleries

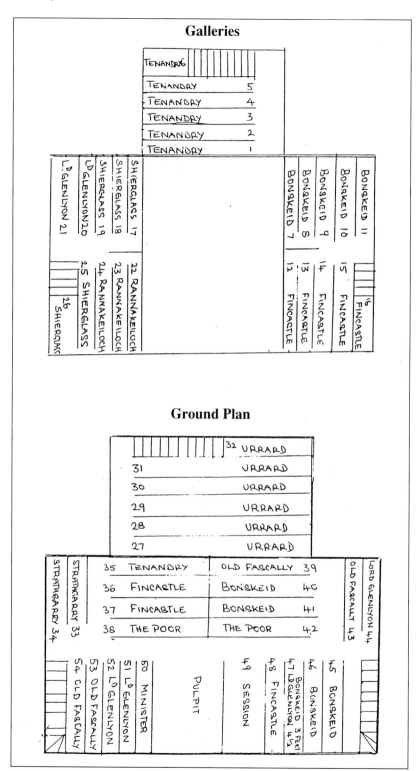

Ground Plan

Ground plan and galleries of Tenandry church as drawn up in 1837. (Courtesy of Lady Barbour)

	Blair	Moulin	Dull	Total
Tenandry	107			107
Fincastle			138	138
Bonskeid, Borenich	69		93	162
Shierglas			49	49
Strathgarry		14		14
Urrard		94		94
Reinakyllich	17			17
Old Faskally		60		60
Orchillbeg, Pitdornie	___	95	15	110
	193	263	295	751

Later, presbytery pointed out that Borenich had never been in Blair Atholl parish and had always belonged to Dull.

The Hays' choice for the first minister of Tenandry was the Reverend Ferguson, minister of the Gaelic chapel in Perth, and although he at first agreed to take up the appointment, later withdrew his acceptance. James Hay therefore nominated William Grant, born in Nairn in 1806 and educated at King's College, Aberdeen and Edinburgh University.[11] He had been assistant to the minister in Ardersier for three years and came to Tenandry with his stipend set at £85 a year. He was ordained and inducted on 15 September 1836 in the presence of members of Dunkeld Presbytery when he was: ". . . by prayer and imposition of hands solemnly set apart to the office of this Holy Trinity, the Brethren giving him the right hand of fellowship."[12]

By the Declamatory Enactments for Chapels of Ease, dated 31 May 1834, William Grant was entitled to be a member of presbytery and synod and therefore eligible to sit in the General Assembly of the Church of Scotland, thus placing him on the same standing as other ministers.

Although still part of Blair Atholl parish, Tenandry was established as a "territorial district" and five local ministers were appointed to assist the new minister in the constitution of a kirk session and the ordaining of elders. The first kirk session meeting was held on 15 September 1836 when the Reverend Duncan Campbell, minister of Moulin, was appointed session clerk. An elder was appointed from each of the three parishes and they were: Donald Ferguson, Balrobbie (Blair Atholl); John Stewart, Orchill (Moulin) and Peter Forbes, Milton of Fincastle, (Dull).[13]

Elder's Affray
At a kirk session meeting in November 1839, the minister referred:

> . . . with sorrow to a gross outrage which had been committed in this parish
> on Saturday 9th current by two of the parishioners Donald Ferguson residing
> at Balrobbie and Thomas Robertson at Ardtulichan, the former an elder, who
> quarrelled and fought with sticks and fists, which rendered official interposition
> necessary and on which punishment by fine and imprisonment ensued.[14]

As one of the offenders was an elder, the kirk session referred the matter to presbytery, who recommended they summon him to appear before the session on 5 January, "to answer to his scandalous conduct of fighting". Donald Ferguson refused to appear on that day, saying it was a Sabbath and when he finally appeared on 13 January, he at once "confessed with shame and sorrow"

*Interior of
Tenandry church.*

that he was guilty of fighting and was summoned to appear before presbytery on 18 February.

On that day he was charged with having fought with another parishioner on the Saturday before Communion Day and stated in his defence that he had been driven to it by "gross and violent provocation". He was therefore suspended from all his duties an an elder. The case came to court, when both men were fined £2 and bound over by the sheriff to keep the peace. Presbytery instructed the kirk session to summon witnesses for a deposition on 15 April but found this was not possible because Ferguson was jailed by his creditors on 13 April. Some of the witnesses were reluctant to give evidence against him because he was a neighbour and this would "agitate the affair anew and would stir up most disagreeable feelings in the district".

Two years later Ferguson asked to have the suspension lifted and his church privilges restored, so the session:

> . . . in consideration of the propper and becoming behaviour of the said Donald Ferguson of late and his regularity in attending public worship, acceded to his desire, waiving the question of restoration to the eldership which he said he had no wish to exercise.[15]

The collection in 1840 came to £14.6.9, of which £7.1.3. was given to the General Assembly Education Scheme, £3.3.2 to the India Mission, £2.1.3 to Church Extension and £2.1.1 to Colonial Churches. A year later the collection had more than doubled to £32.15.0, which was disposed of as follows: Education £8; Church Extension £7.17.6; India Mission £5.1.0; Conversion of Jews £5.10.0; Colonial Churches £3.1.6 and Perth Infirmary £3.5.0.[16]

Minister Secedes

During May 1843, the Reverend William Grant left the established church to join the Free Church but continued to use Tenandry manse and church, although the latter was restricted to weekday usage and Sundays avoided. His last service in Tenandry was a Harvest Thanksgiving, which was held on a Thursday. However the SSPCK continued to pay his salary and according to William Young, presbytery lawyer, as they had never acknowledged the authority of the General Assembly to interfere with any of its proceedings, "still less would they hold that Presbytery was entitled to depose or remove one of their teachers". He further observed that there was a difference of opinion within that Society as to whether they should maintain their association with the Established Church.[17]

By December, William Grant was still using the church for services but plans were being made to apply for an interdict against him to vacate the premises. As the church, in the eyes of presbytery, had been vacant for more than six months, they gave very careful consideration to exercising their right to nominate a new minister, although the founders themselves had been searching desperately for a successor. This was minuted at a meeting on 19 December 1843:

> . . . considering that the said Mr Grant was declared to be no longer a minister of the Established Church of Scotland by a sentence of the General Assembly on 24 of May last . . . the patrons of said church or chapel of Tenandry have failed effectually to exercise their right of nomination to the same . . . the right of nomination to the same is now vested in them [presbytery] and they resolve now to exercise said right accordingly.[18]

About this time the founders considered they had found a suitable applicant, the Reverend Alexander McIntyre, from Edinburgh, whom Christian Hay felt to be:

> . . . a pastor who will devote himself to the work of the ministry as one that must give account in that day when all hearts are laid open, and when the high and honourable office of Christian pastor will appear in brightness . . . Mr McIntyre's steady rejection of many better offers confirms my humble hope that he is appointed by God for Tenandry.[19]

Presbytery considered that Alexander McIntyre was "eminently fitted to discharge the pastoral duties of said church or chapel efficiently and acceptably" and decided to back his nomination.[20] However McIntyre had reservations about the post, one worry being meeting the presbytery, as he asked the Reverend Dr Irvine, the Blair Atholl minister, to tell him "what I am likely to be examined upon". Other doubts concerned the job itself, as he confided in a letter to the minister that:

> Tenandry holds out a very different prospect – a very gloomy one – the directors of the Society are nearly divided between the Established and Free church . . . I learn that almost all the parishioners have subscribed their names to come out with Mr Grant.

The letter concluded with his thanks for the support of Mrs Hay, "an excellent lady who has met with so much unprovoked and undeserved ill usage from Mr Grant".[21] There is no evidence that Alexander McIntyre accepted the post and the substance of this letter would seem to corroborate this.

The Reverend Dr Irvine received several letters from William Grant, in one of which he outlined his plan to: ". . . make out a case of oppression against the Presbytery and me [Irvine] which may enable him, at least, to send some exaggerated statement to the witness. As he has no handle for anything of this kind in truth, I shall endeavour to prevent him from getting any thro' his correspondence with me." The presbytery's interdict for Grant to remove himself from Tenandry was served and the keys were finally handed over in December 1843. As Tenandry was thus without a minister, Dr Irvine sought presbytery's approval to bring in a probationer to take services in English, but only until a Gaelic-speaking minister could be found, and this was approved.[22]

Quoad Sacra Parish

In April 1850 Dunkeld Presbytery discussed a proposal put forward by the Reverend Dr Irvine to convert the Tenandry Chapel of Ease into a *quoad sacra* parish. There were at least two good reasons for the vacancy remaining unfilled. Firstly, the stipend had remained at £85 and secondly, as long as Tenandry was part of Blair Atholl parish, no Tenandry minister was in charge of his own destiny. The following propositions were therefore submitted:

1. That the Assembly Committee should contribute an additional £150 to the endowment fund.
2. That the Society (SSPCK) should transfer £350 from the repair fund, as with no stipend, this had accumulated over the years. This would add £500 to the endowment, making that fund £2,100.
3. That the Society would agree to give 5% interest and continue the additional £5 to make a stipend of £110.

The SSPCK agreed to these propositions as the outcome of such actions "would be highly conducive to the moral and religious interests of the inhabitants residing in the district".[23]

The plan to form a *quoad sacra* parish was based on:

> An Act to facilitate the disjoining or dividing of extensive or populous parishes and the erecting of new parishes in that part of the United Kingdom called Scotland. (1843)

This act stipulated that a district could be designated a *quoad sacra* parish, which was separated from those parishes, in this case three, from which it was formed. These proposals were to be advertised in the *Edinburgh Gazette* or other appropriate Edinburgh newspapers.

It also stipulated that a stipend was to be set at no less that £100 a year or seven chalders of oatmeal and a suitable house and offices. Where no manse was available, the stipend was £120 or eight and a quarter chalders. The county sheriff was responsible for ensuring that a tenth of seats were free and a fifth let at a suitable rent agreed by presbytery. The remainder were to be leased at the discretion of the minister, for defraying expenses of the precentor and beadle. One free pew was reserved for the minister's family and another for officiating elders. The minister and elders of a *quoad sacra* parish were to enjoy all the status, power, rights and privileges of a parish minister and elders in the Church of Scotland.[24]

Parish Boundary

Among the plans and documents submitted for the formation of this *quoad sacra* parish was a description of the new boundary:

The new parish to extend from the east march of the Athole Estate on the bank of Loch Tummel downwards along the banks of the lake and the rivers Tummel and Garry at Invergarry, thence along the south bank of the Garry upwards to the west march of the Estate of Shierglas where it bounds the Athole Estate and thence southwards following the line of march between the Athole Estate in the one hand and the lands of Shierglas, Fincastle and Borennich on the other till the above mentioned march of the Athole lands on Loch Tummel is reached. On the north side of the Garry the new parish to extend from the burn of Aldeachan to the west of the Toll bar of Killicrankie, northwards to the burn of Aldclune, embracing the whole of the parish of Moulin above the Pass of Killicrankie, with the farm of Rinnancaolach in the Parish of Blair Athole, and the lands of Baillephuirt in the Parish of Dull.[25]

According to the Moulin and Tenandry Parish Magazine for September 1902, the boundary towards Pitlochry was uncertain. The march appears to be a dyke at the end of the lands of Old Faskally, then following the Tighnateid Burn but thereafter taking an obscure line down to the old ferry called Baillephuirt. On the south side of the River Garry, the last house near the west march is Garrybank Cottage, opposite the footbridge, while Chapelton of Borenich forms the boundary to the south, beside Loch Tummel.[26]

The new parish embraced the following lands:

Borenich on Loch Tummel and Coillebrochain – property of Glas Sandeman;
Tenandry belonging to Mrs Hay;
Reinakyllich owned by Colonel Robert Richardson;
Fincastle, the property of Mr R C Colquhoun;
Bonskeid owned by Glas Sandeman;
Pitdornie part of the Atholl estate;
Shierglas belonging to Mr William McInroy;
Baillephuirt the property of Mr Archibald Butter;
Strathgarry owned by Mr Allan Stewart;
Orchillbeg part of Atholl estate;
Urrard the property of Miss Alston Stewart;
Old Faskally and Druid belonging to Mr Archibald Butter.[27]

Glebe Land

Mrs Hay assigned six acres of land to form the glebe:

All and whole that piece of land consisting of six acres or thereby with the church or chapel dwelling house or manse and offices and appurtinances erected by the said Mrs Christian Craigie Stewart or Hay all enclosed by a stone wall or dry stone dyke.[28]

Another five acres of pasture land were made over to the church which comprised:

. . . all and whole the row of cottages adjoining the said manse of Tenandry consisting of dwelling house and stable to be used in all time coming as a dwelling house for the church officers and a stable for the convenience of those coming from a distance to church, together with the garden attached together with the piece of pasture land behind and above said cottages consisting of about five acres or thereby as enclosed by a boundary wall recently erected. . . .[29]

As part of the conversion to *quoad sacra* status, the church and surrounding property was valued in August 1850:[30]

Value of Church		
Mason work	£185. 0. 0	
Plumber work	45. 0. 0	
Carpenter, plasterer and glazier work	261. 5. 0	
Bell	10. 0. 0	
		£501. 5. 0
Value of Manse		
Mason work	£110. 0. 0	
Slater, plumber work	3. 0. 0	
Carpenter, plasterer and glazier work	107. 8. 0	
		£250.18. 0
Value of detached Offices		
Barn, Stable and fuel shed	32. 0. 0	
Beadle's house and stable	48. 0. 0	
Enclosure wall of added ground	12. 0. 0	
		£92. 0. 0
Total		£844. 3. 0

Tenandry was formally constituted into a *quoad sacra* parish, being designated "Church and Parish of Tenandry" on 9 July 1851.

By this time a minister had been chosen. Patrick Grant, born in Cromdale in 1821, was the son of James and Jane Grant and was educated at Aberdeen University, becoming an ordained minister on 17 April 1851. He died unmarried in 1889, having served Tenandry church for thirty eight years and is buried in the churchyard there. A stone erected by his parishioners bears a testimonial to his "learning, piety and faithfulness". He has been described as:

Tenandry manse opposite the church.

... a man of the purest life of the most fervent faith and of a singularly spiritual mind. He possessed great natural ability and left behind a book recently published called *The Augenic* [Eugenic] *Declension*, a record of his researches.[31]

Christian Hay, one of the founders of Tenandry church, was born on 9 July 1778, a daughter of James Stewart of Urrard. She died on 3 November 1860 and there is a polished red granite tablet to her memory inside St Brides church, the traditional burial place of her ancestors.

Patrick Grant was succeeded by the Reverend John Anderson Robertson, ordained to Tenandry on 14 May 1889. During his first year he was asked to leave his stable door open on Sundays "as was the custom" for the use of the congregation. (In the 1930s this stable was converted into a garage.) He left Tenandry in 1903 to go to St Anne's Church in Corstorphine, Edinburgh. William Goldie Boag, ordained to Tenandry in 1903, was born in Polmont in September 1868, the only son of William Goldie Boag, minister of Delting in Shetland and studied at Edinburgh University. He married Elizabeth, daughter of James Stewart Johnston, minister of Cambuslang in 1903, died on 3 September 1914 and is buried in Tenandry churchyard.

John Lamb, born in September 1858, was the next minister, educated at Aberdeen Grammar School and Aberdeen University, where he graduated MA in 1878. From 1878-1886 he was a schoolmaster in the parish of Forglen, Banffshire, passed his BD in 1888 and was ordained as a Missionary Professor in the General Assembly's Institution, Calcutta on 15 June 1890. He came as the Tenandry minister in 1913 where he remained until 1922.[32]

He was followed by the Reverend Donald MacBean in 1923, who left in 1935 to join the united parish of Logie Easter in Ross-shire and his place was taken by Duncan Sinclair from 1935 to 1953. In 1954, when Gordon Makins filled the vacancy, the parish was linked with Foss and Tummel. When he left in 1958 he was succeeded by Harold Meredith (1959-1967) and then Hamish Walker (1968-1976). The following year the link with Foss was severed and in that year it seemed that Tenandry might be united with the Pitlochry congregation. That scheme foundered, as did a later plan to link up with Blair Atholl and Struan parish in 1995. Tenandry then received permission to have a *locum tenens* in James Fuller, who stayed for two years. In 1981 it was designated as a "continuing

Tilt marble baptismal font in Tenandry church.

vacancy", first under the charge of the Reverend Bill Shannon, Moulin and West Church, Pitlochry and then from 1983 to the present time (1998), under Sir Robin Barbour.[33]

In 1884 the offer of a harmonium from the Butter sisters, living in Faskally House, was accepted by the session. They had expressed a desire to "assist in conducting the psalmody" and this offer was to be free of any expense to the congregation as long as they lived. The two ladies took charge of the music and played for many years until their brother, Archibald died, and they left the area. Before they went away they agreed to pay £6 a year to the new organist, Mr Kellock, the local schoolmaster, "provided he takes a real and hearty interest it it and provides a competent substitute during his vacation". The session added another £4 to make the annual organist's fees up to £10.[34]

A beadle was appointed in 1890 and a cottage was built nearby for him. For £2 a year and free accommodation, he was responsible for the upkeep of the church and graveyard. Major repairs to the church were undertaken in 1896, when it was re-floored, seating renewed and the pulpit altered at a cost of £170.15.0. In 1916 the graveyard was enlarged while the roof was repaired in 1919. Major alterations to the church were made in 1939 when the west entrance was closed and a vestry built on that side. The pulpit, communion table, organ and choir were repositioned on the south side of the church.[35]

Tenandry church still stands after 150 years, and its parishioners, though now reduced in numbers, still continue to worship there as an active and independent congregation.[36]

References

1. BCCR Trunk 45 (9) 77
2. BCCR Trunk 46 (1) 152
3. BCCR Trunk 46 (1) 224
4. BCCR Trunk 9 V 6
5. SRO CH 2 106/15
6. SRO CH 2 106/16
7. PSAS Volume 122
8. *Tenandry Kirk,* Barbour
9. TKSM
10. Ibid
11. *Fasti,* Scott
12. SRO CH 2 106/16
13. Ibid
14. TKSM
15. Ibid
16. SRO CH 2 106/16
17. J I R
18. SRO CH 2 106/16
19. J I R
20. SRO CH 2 106/16
21. J I R
22. SRO CH 2 106/17
23. Ibid
24. Ibid
25. Ibid
26 Strathgarry Papers
27. SRO CH 2 106/17
28. Ibid
29. Ibid
30. TKSM
31. Ibid
32. *Fasti,* Scott
33. *Tenandry Kirk*, Barbour
34. TKSM
35. Ibid
36. *Tenandry Kirk*, Barbour

eleven

The Free Church

The General Assembly of 1842 marked a watershed in the history of the Church of Scotland when a motion "that patronage is the main cause of the evils in which the church is involved and ought to be abolished", was carried by a large majority. Many believed that the church had strayed too far from the precepts of Calvinist presbyterianism into the hands of landlords and an accompanying system of patronage. The "Day of Disruption" was on 18 May 1843, when 474 ministers of the Church of Scotland seceded to form the new Free Church of Scotland. It was clearly felt to be a time for a church of "purity, clarity and freedom" and these ideals formed the basis of the Free Church.

Glen Fincastle Chapel

Mrs Margaret Stewart Sandeman of Bonskeid and Springland, Perth, became a member of the Free church in May 1843, and received the following letter from the Reverend William Grant of Tenandry in December of that year:

Glen Fincastle chapel, built in 1844.

. . . I must inform you that an interdict has been served on me and that I have delivered up the keys of the church. Our strong expectations of retaining the church as having been a chapel of ease belonging to the Society for Propagating Christian Knowledge, are now at an end. We worshipped yesterday (24th December) in the open air, a day unusually fine, and I intend being here also next Sabbath, if the Lord will. I had the tent on the glebe last Sabbath, but as Mr Niven [presbytery clerk] is to be in Tenandry chapel next Lord's Day, I don't like to be so near. On this account I write to ask permission to put the tent in your park or birch wood at a little distance from the house. . . .

I am almost single-handed in this country. We have had no permanent relief sent as yet. From Sabbath morning to the following Sabbath night, I sometimes ride one hundred and fifty miles, and after all cannot undertake the third of the work.[1]

When Mrs Sandeman read this letter she expressed surprise to her ground officer that people were worshipping in the open air, asked him to consult with the minister about the most suitable place for the tent and expressed the hope that "a convenient and sheltered place will be found". She made plans to build a small chapel on her land at the foot of Glen Fincastle and it was ready in 1844. It bears a small inscription of the founder's initials – M S S 1843 above the entrance. The wooden belfry houses a 14-inch diameter steel bell and although there is is no foundry mark, it was almost certainly cast by Naylor Vickers & Co of Sheffield.[2]

Mrs Sandeman's intention was to provide a place of worship for those in Tenandry parish who had joined the Free Church. No real congregation was formed, however, possibly because ownership of the chapel remained with the family and thus it was perhaps perceived as not being truly "free". Many former parishioners became members of the Free Church in Pitlochry or Blair Atholl.

After only a year, William Grant left Glen Fincastle to become the Free Church minister in Moulin until 1847, when he moved to Perth to become minister of the Free Gaelic Church. He emigrated to Australia in 1853, where he became the minister at Shoalhaven, New South Wales, until his death in 1897.[3]

Services were held in the chapel in summer until 1886 and occasional ones in winter until 1890, when the Reverend John Robertson, the Tenandry Church of Scotland minister, held services there once a month. After this time it became a more regular place of worship for parishioners living in the west side of the parish beside Loch Tummel and for twenty five years, weekly services were taken by the Tenandry minister and the Blair Atholl Free Church minister.

The chapel was also used for a time as a school. The local school, which at one time used a room to the rear of Fincastle Post Office, transferred to the chapel and remained a voluntary school until the new Education Act of 1919, when it was taken over by the County Education Authority.[4]

The chapel celebrated its centenary on 14 September 1944, when the Very Reverend Professor John Baillie, Principal of New College, Edinburgh, was the preacher. Glen Fincastle Chapel is still owned by Mrs Sandeman's descendants and services are held on Sundays in the summer months, with a communion service once a year.

Island Church

On 13 February 1843, three months before the Disruption, a group of people met in Blair Atholl church where they resolved to form a congregation of the Free

Church. The guiding hand through the early stages of forming this congregation was Atholl Stuart, born on 19 February 1818 and ordained as a minister in 1844. He was a son of John Stewart, the Blair Atholl parish minister, who had allowed him to use the church for the meeting. This action was vigorously opposed by a large landowner in the parish, who, within a few days of the meeting, petitioned the County Sheriff to call the parish minister summarily before him and forbid him from allowing such a meeting ever again within the church.

However John Stewart was a very infirm old man and he died within six weeks. He was buried in Blair Atholl churchyard, which because of the amount of gravel and boulders, needed a retaining wall to prevent the grave collapsing. Within three days of the interment, the family was served with a writ, stipulating that the wall which surrounded the grave should be taken down. Failure to comply would result in the complainer arranging for the work to be done and sending in an account for it. Such was the general uproar and indignation at the prospect of the minister's grave being disturbed, that the attempt was given up. Matters did not even rest there, however, as a year later an attempt was made to claim the costs of the writ that had been issued.[5]

The "large landowner" mentioned in the records as the instigator of this affront, was undoubtedly the 2nd Lord Glenlyon, (who became the 6th Duke of Atholl in 1846). For the first twenty four years of his ministry in Blair Atholl, John Stewart had served under the 4th Duke and the events of the attempted suppression of Struan church would indicate that he was very much in the duke's pocket. All this changed in 1837 when the 2nd Lord Glenlyon succeeded his father and was later the prime mover in trying to eradicate the presence of the Free Church in Atholl.

Open-Air Services

After the Disruption, a number of tenants invited the Free Church congregation to use their land for open-air services, when public worship was conducted from a tent provided for the minister. Some heritors were strongly opposed to this and as soon as a tent was erected, would have it knocked down, with the threat of "legal prosecution and with the most disagreeable consequences", if they permitted use of their land again.

All this while, many heritors were demanding that the "Free Church must be put down" and every time a writ was issued, it incurred legal costs. The minister steadfastly refused to pay them, preferring "in the furnace of affliction, to go to prison rather than face financial ruin". Atholl Stuart actively supported his father in his duties as a minister and refused to comply with requests to suppress the new movement. The congregation decided to dispense with preaching tents and every Sunday changed the venue of the service according to circumstances. Like the covenanters in the past, they met in remote parts of the parish.

Just downstream from its confluence with the River Tilt, the River Garry at one time curved through what is now the golf course, until it reached the Craggan Corner, where it divided to form King's Island. Also known as Shierglas Island, but now land-locked, it was at the time of the Disruption, part of Shierglas estate to which it was linked by a ferry. Traditionally its name

Preaching tent for the Free church minister to conduct open-air services.

PREACHING TENT.

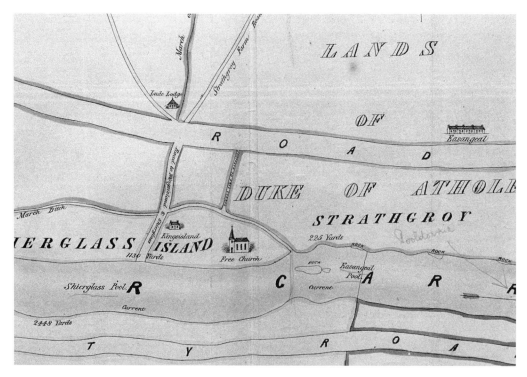

Map of "Shierglass Island" showing the location of the Free Church.

has been connected with Robert the Bruce who is said to have camped there at the start of the fourteenth century, on his way to Rannoch.[6]

At the eastern end of the 'island' there is a "beautiful spot surrounded with weeping birches and other woods of indigenous growth". The tenant, whose name was William (possibly Ferguson) and nicknamed "King William" for his Free Church sympathies, allowed the congregation to erect a temporary meeting house there and was observed "industriously and determinedly cutting down and clearing away the underwood which grew upon the place". The manager of the local sawmill was forbidden to supply any timber for this project but, on hearing of their plight, the Marquis of Breadalbane offered not only to provide sufficient wood from Taymouth but also to deliver it. Work on the wooden structure, known as the Island Church, began in November 1843 and was completed the following February.

Opposition

Opposition to the Free Church grew amongst the landowners, who had not given up the idea of suppressing it. Between the island church and the road there was a strip of land, less than twenty yards wide, which was crossed by a footpath. This ground was owned by a hostile landowner who issued instructions that all access over this ground was forbidden. He went on to say that: "I trust therefore, that any further attempt to occupy the footpath will be abandoned, as the refusal to do so will assuredly lead to the adoption of disagreeable measures . . .".

On one balmy June Sabbath the congregation approached the church as usual, only to be greeted by a notice which read "No Road This Way" and a stranger, employed by the proprietor, who had been stationed there to record the name of anyone who passed. This caused the congregation to take a more circuitous route to the church but, strange to relate, the stranger died suddenly only a few days later in "peculiar circumstances" and access to the church was never again challenged.

Although a comfortable site for worship in dry weather, the ground was low-lying and subject to frequent flooding in winter. Yet, despite being constantly cut off by water, there was only one instance in the thirteen years of the church's existence, when a service could not be held. On that occasion there had been unusually heavy and continuous rain during the night and the following morning the church appeared – "planted as it were, in the midst of the great waters".[7]

Kirk Session

The first meeting of the Free Church kirk session was held on 9 June 1844, with the Reverend Atholl Stuart presiding and Robert Robertson, teacher at Struan school, appointed session clerk. Because of this, he and his young family were ejected from their home despite the resistance and anger of the SSPCK who were patrons of the school. In 1848 the session decided that communion, normally held twice a year, should take place on the same days as the Established church. Their reasoning was that many of their members were employed by the Duke of Atholl and were unable to get time off on both Free and Established church communion days. It appeared that "masters and others frequently refused liberty to their servants who were Free Church people to keep the Free Church fast days". Samuel Robertson and Charles Robertson were therefore asked to make such arrangements as necessary and to have the summer communion in July. Regarding winter, they were to "take care that no [communion] Sabbath be agreed upon unless it will always be a Sabbath on which there will be good moonlight".[8]

Services also took place in Bridge of Bruar to cater for those people living in the west side of the parish and in 1848 the session recorded that: "The Gaelic school opened at Fendar Bridge was violently closed by the Duke of Atholl". It was common knowledge that the 6th Duke, formerly Lord Glenlyon, was strongly opposed to the Free Church and it was assumed that this closure was instigated by the Established church minister, the Reverend Dr Irvine, "who dreaded the well-known influence of a Gaelic schoolmaster in the parish". The school thereafter met in a barn but the factor ordered the tenant, Alexander Stewart in Runroy, to stop allowing his premises to be used as a school. It was reported that the teacher, William Campbell, who had previously been in charge of the Glen Garry school, had been unable to find another post and "is meanwhile idle". All this was part of a plan "of sweeping the Free church out of Atholl".

The ravages of the weather, constant flooding and "the sapping operations of a multitude of rabbits which burrow below its foundations and floors", had seriously undermined the Island church, rendering it unsafe. The need for an alternative site was paramount and one was offered by the wife of the laird of Strathgarry, which lay in a detached part of Moulin parish, and she wrote: "I am a member of the Free Church;

The "No Road This Way" sign near the Island Church.

The Island Church after a sudden spate.

THE PRESENT FREE CHURCH OF BLAIR ATHOLL.

but had I been what I was, an Episcopalian, I could not refuse my fellow Christians such a request".[9]

The River Garry was however, too hazardous a barrier for the bulk of the congregation who would have required a ferry for safe passage.

St Andrews Free Church

In May 1855 the session agreed to contact Mr McInroy, the laird of Lude about acquiring a site in Bridge of Tilt and wrote to him, outlining the situation:

1. That the wooden building on the Island of Shierglas is decaying rapidly and is now unsafe.
2. That repeated applications for a site have been made to the Duke of Atholl and in every instance his reply has been "certainly not".
3. That the office bearers ask you to grant them a site for a church.

James McInroy indicated that as several of the objections he had in the past no longer applied, he was prepared to offer a site on the following conditions:

1. That a situation could be agreed that presented no objections to him and was convenient to the session.
2. That he would approve the plan and materials for building the church. It had to be kept in good order and when not required as a place of worship, would revert to the proprietors of Lude. No other building was to be erected on the ground and the church only used as a place of worship or Sunday School.
3. The church and ground was to be disposed of with the proprietor's consent in writing.
4. The ground around the church was to be kept neatly and enclosed with a stone and lime dyke surmounted with coping stones.
5. No part of the ground could be used as a burial ground or graveyard.
6. The annual feu of the ground was to be at the usual rate and he was to be relieved of all expenses concerning the transfer.[10]

The session recorded their satisfaction and gratitude at obtaining a site and the minister agreed to contact James McInroy about the most suitable place. The chosen location was beside the road in Bridge of Tilt and a feu charter was drawn up in favour of the Reverend Atholl Stuart and his elders: Neil McGlashan, tailor, Bailentoul; Charles Stewart, shoemaker, Fraochran; Samuel Robertson, farmer and innkeeper, Bruar; Robert Douglas, shoemaker, Invervack and Alexander Stewart, farmer, Grenich:

All and whole that piece of ground being part of the field lying to the southeast of the Village of Bridge of Tilt presently possessed by William Reid Smith as tenant and to the south of the turnpike road from Perth to Inverness, along the said turnpike road southwards 60 yards or thereby and which is bounded as follows: On the north by the said turnpike road, on the west by a road about twenty feet wide leading from the said road towards the Fraochran and on the east and south of the said fields which subjects extend to sixty six falls of ground or thereby. . . .[11]

The perimeter wall was to be 4½ feet high and the feu duty was set at £8.5.0 a year.

Straitened Finances

The finances of the Blair Atholl Free Church congregation were in a parlous state. The refusal of sites had incurred a loss of £350 through writs; the Island Church had cost at least £400 to build and was now worth at most £60. The parishioners, comprising mainly of tenants of small upland farms, crofters, tradesmen, labourers and servants had raised only £300 in funds for the new church and had received a grant of £112.10.0 from the Building Committee of the Free Church towards an estimated cost of £1,800. The minister observed: "The congregation will be thrown into the unhappy position of being hindered for a long period of years with a heavy debt . . .".[12]

St Andrews Free Church was completed in 1857 and named after a chapel dedicated to St Andrew, situated on the east bank of the River Tilt, as recorded in the first Statistical Account of Scotland:

On the east bank of the Tilt, which falls into the Garry, south-east of Atholl-house, is Clagh-Ghil-Aindreas, or the cemetery of St Andrew's disciple. What the Tilt has left of it, is a part of a circle; many of the bones are entire but crumble to pieces when touched. The coffins are composed of five flags each, and seem to have been used, to save the trouble of making wooden coffins, or probably to preserve the corps from the wolves.

St Andrews Free Church built in Bridge of Tilt in 1857.

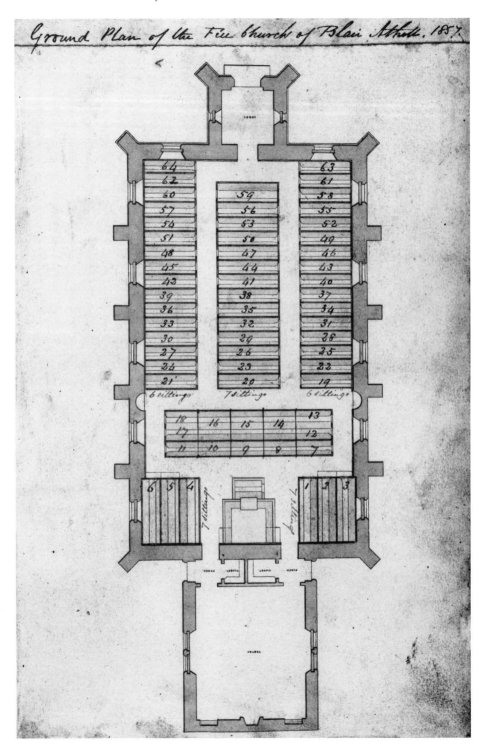

1857 seating plan of Blair Atholl Free Church. (Scottish Record Office CH3/358/4).

The site of the local Andrewsmas Market, held on St Andrews Day, 30 November, was a little to the south of here and a white stone on a raised bank, which remained in existence until the middle of the eighteenth century, was used as the market cross.

The new church measured 65 feet by 35 feet, excluding the tower and vestry. It had five windows flanked by buttresses, a lobby under the pinnacled tower on the north end and a vestry at the southern end. It was built to hold nearly 400 people at 18 inches per seat and had no galleries. There were three blocks of pews in the well of the church which accommodated 290 people – 98 in the central block of 14 pews, flanked by two rows each of 16 pews, for 192 sittings. There were 12 pews, each of 4 sitters, immediately in front of the pulpit, which was flanked on both sides by three, each with seven places. Behind the pulpit were two closets which backed on to the vestry.[13] The tower held the bell which had a diameter of 32 inches and was marked – C & G MEARS FOUNDERS LONDON 1857, having been cast in Whitechapel Foundry, East London. [14]

Seating Regulations
Seating Rules and Regulations were set out by the Deacons' Court:

1. Pews and seats to be allocated among members and adherents of the Free church and any remaining to be distributed among those belonging to other churches who apply for them.
2. Priority of application will have preference and if more than one is for the same pew, this will be divided by lot.
3. No person will occupy more than one seat 18 inches wide in any pew to the exclusion of others who may desire a seat either "habitually or occasionally".
4. No one will be allowed to hold seats unless they are occupied regularly.
5. Rows one to six and fifty nine are declared principal seats and are reserved under the special control of the Deacons' Court. Rates for the other pews and seats were as follows:

   I   Individuals paid a uniform rate of one shilling.

   II   The rates for families were -

i	Sitting	One shilling
ii	Sittings	One shilling and sixpence
iii	Sittings	Two shillings
iv	Sittings	Two shillings and sixpence
v	Sittings	Three shillings
vi	Sittings	Three shillings and sixpence
		and sixpence per additional one.

6. Free seats will be granted to people receiving parochial relief or are unable to pay through poverty.
7. Anyone rejected from a seat will only pay a proportion of the rent in relation to the period of time it was occupied.[15]

When the church opened, the principal seats were allocated thus:
Pew 1.   Minister through not needing it, gave it to Elders.
Pew 2.   Minister, presented it as a gift to Rev. A. Smart.
Pew 3.   Mr Stewart, Strathgarry and Mr Graham, Bonskeid.
Pew 4.   The Deacons.
Pew 5.   Ann Stewart, Killiecrankie and Alexander Douglas, Bridge of Tilt.
Pew 6.   George Barbour, Bonskeid.
Pew 59.   James McInroy, Laird of Lude.

Pew 30 was allocated to William Ferguson of King's Island, possibly "King William", the tenant who had given part of his land for the Island Church in 1843. In December 1857, Charles McAra from Kincraigie, who shared pew 28 with Robert Stewart, asked to move to another six-seat pew which he could share with his neighbour, John Stewart, Croftmore. The following month, Ann Stewart, Middlebridge, then in pew 57, asked to move into the middle of the church but no further forward than pew 41, seven rows from the back. Pews 15 and 16, right in front of the pulpit, were free and for the poor, while three seats in pew 53 were given to Robert Robertson for his services as precentor.[16] The collection for 1857-1858 amounted to £12.13.10, to which the largest contributors were George Barbour, Bonskeid, with £1.10.0 and James McInroy, Lude, with £1.0.0.

The Reverend Atholl Stuart, who lived in Middlebridge, resigned in 1882 and there is still a memorial plaque to him on the former vestry wall which reads:

> He upheld its cause amidst many difficulties, preaching in the open air during the years of the disruption and afterwards at King's Island in a wooden erection known as the "Island Church". He laboured earnestly and increasingly for the good of his people until ill-health caused him to resign on 30 March 1882 and he died on 13 September 1894.

He is buried beside his father in Blair Atholl churchyard, having been the Free Church minister for nearly forty years, guiding his congregation through the turbulence of the Disruption, a time when no other district encountered more determined and bitter opposition. In 1857 he printed a book for private circulation:

Blair Atholl as it Was and Is
or
A SHORT AND INTERESTING NARRATIVE
of the
PAST HISTORY AND PRESENT CONDITION
of the
Free Church in Blair Atholl

> It is moral beauty, when found along with natural beauty, that makes the latter inexpressibly pleasing to a sanctified mind, and gives it to a parish distinguished for both a twofold claim to be called a garden of the Lord. . . . The promotion and increase of the moral and spiritual beauty of Blair Atholl is the purpose which the following narrative is intended to secure. . . .
>
> Atholl Stuart

Free Church Manse

For ten years from 1882, the Reverend Alexander Bain was the Free church minister, and the question of a manse for him arose early on. This matter had been brought up in 1857 by Atholl Stuart, who said then – "There is no suitable house in the whole district for the Minister". The session agreed that if it was not possible to secure a site outwith the church grounds, then the laird should be approached about building within the existing enclosure. The letter to him from the minister stressed that such a building ". . . so far from detracting in any way from the beauty of the surroundings, would considerably enhance the same . . .".

The laird, William McInroy, agreed to a manse being built on the site, ". . . on condition it was used solely for that purpose" and his letter continued:

. . . and in the event of circumstances arising hereafter to cause the authorities to wish to dispense with it as a manse, I or my successor in possession of the Estate shall have power to take possession at a valuation of the materials, such valuation not to exceed the original cost of the buildings.

Existing charges were to remain unchanged but he declined to incur any expense in introducing water to the manse. His factor, Mr Christie, was asked to have an agreement drawn up "without the intervention of lawyers".[17]

In 1884 an estimate of £2.16.0 from Mr Miller in Pitlochry, for painting and puttying the windows was obtained and accepted. He was also asked to clean the windows after the work was completed and if that task had not been included in his estimate, then a small additional sum was to be allowed. The necessity of painting the pews and improving the lighting was discussed as there had been complaints about the condition of both. It was agreed that "The erection of standards and lamps for the better lighting of the area of the church in the winter months" would be attended to and the matter of the state of the pews would have to wait until the following year.[18]

Alexander Bain left the area in 1892 and he was succeeded by the Reverend Alexander Matheson, who stayed for six years, to be followed by John Simpson, who was ordained in St Andrews in March 1899, emigrating to Woodstock, South Africa, three years later. After spending seven years at Tummel Bridge Free Church, Hugh MacCallum was appointed to St Andrews in 1903, until his death in 1920 and is buried in Blair Atholl churchyard. He was followed by Alexander Anderson Strathearn who was born in Kirriemuir in 1879 and graduated MA from St Andrews University in 1903. After serving in Stranraer he was inducted to Cargill in 1909, transferred to Liff, Angus in 1915 and finally to Blair Atholl in 1920.[19]

In 1900 a large majority of the Free Church Assembly voted to join up with the United Presbyterian Church, together becoming the United Free Church. A minority supported the *status quo*, leading to six years of wrangling over property and funds of the Free Church. St Andrews became part of the United Free and remained so until 1929 when it merged with the Established church to form the Church of Scotland. Not only were there now two large churches in the village but also two manses so eventually the manse at Baluain was sold as St Andrews manse was a more conveniently situated home for the parish minister.

In 1950 St Andrews was used as the parish church when Blair Atholl church was renovated and its galleries removed. By 1965 it had been agreed to demolish St Andrews but to retain the tower with its clock as this had been requested by the local council. Two years later the main building was demolished and only the tower left standing but by 1972 it was deemed unsafe and knocked down also. The site of the former church has been landscaped into St Andrews Garden, with lawns, shrubs, trees and garden seats and all that now remains of the Free Church is the small vestry building beside the manse.[20]

Struan Free Church

Within a year of the Disruption, inhabitants in the western end of the parish were petitioning Lord Glenlyon (later the 6th Duke of Atholl) for a site on which to build a Free Church. They maintained that they were "without any place in which to meet for the worship of God, nearer than the church at King's Island . . ." and there were 780 names from residents in Strathtummel, Auchinruidh, Dalreoch,

Glen Garry, Bruar and Calbruar and elsewhere.[21] Samuel Robertson, innkeeper and farmer at Bruar, took pity on them in winter weather, allowing them the use of the inn or his barn.[22]

With no sign of a site being offered, the office-bearers, members and adherents again petitioned the 6th duke:

> Your petitioners are desirous to have a church in which to meet from week to week in the Lord's Day. That at present they are obliged from want of suitable accommodation to meet in a barn which they find to be uncomfortable and unsuitable. That the number of persons adhering to the congregation is 121. Your petitioners earnestly ask of Your Grace a site whereon to build a stone and lime church, or to plant down an iron church which last can be done without breaking the surface.[23]

This, and other similar petitions were either formally refused or left unanswered. There was still no site forthcoming until 1853, when the tenant of Clachan Farm, a member of the established church, allowed them to meet in a nearby wooden shed which had been converted to a temporary homestead. Initially, services were held every third Sunday but within a few years a "missionary", living in Struan, preached there on two consecutive Sundays and the third in Blair Atholl, when the minister would preach in Struan. It began to look as though Struan would never have a permanent Free church building because of the lack of parish finances after building St Andrews and the minister observed that "The congregation will be thrown into the unhappy position of being burdened for a long period of heavy debt and of having to postpone indefinitely the prospect of procuring a church at Struan and a manse . . .".[24]

The wooden building at Clachan of Struan used as a temporary place of worship by Struan Free Church members.

On 19 September 1871, the minister and his three ruling elders petitioned the Free Presbytery of Dunkeld about the plight of their Struan congregation and made the following observations:

> First it is physically impossible for one man ("the minister") to take the oversight in any proper way of a charge so extensive territorially as Blair Athole.
>
> Second the energy of other denominations; the influx of strangers and the altered condition of the country generally render it needful that divine service be in both parishes on <u>every</u> Lord's day.
>
> Third the parish of Struan is a field of labour on which the attention of the church might be somewhat <u>specially</u> bestowed. . . .
>
> Fourth it is a population which is on the increase, of which a good deal might be made.
>
> Fifth there is a congregation now in connection with the Free church of about . . . above fourteen years of age and with the blessing of good and faithful and sustained labour there is the prospect of a congregation which will in due time be raised to the position of a sanction charge.
>
> Sixth the Clachan of Struan is becoming an important locality. The station there belonging to the Highland Railway is a chief (principal) one on the line.[25]

The Minister concluded by pleading that a probationer be appointed to Struan as soon as possible.

Thirty five years after the Disruption, a permanent site was finally obtained, with a feu charter granted by the 7th Duke of Atholl in favour of "Trustees for the Congregation of the body of Christians called the Free Church of Scotland at present worshipping in Struan under leadership of Sutherland". These trustees to whom the charter was given were: The Reverend Archibald Cook Sutherland, Free Church minister of Strathbraan, Dalguise and Struan; Thomas Macdonald, farmer, Auchlany; Malcolm MacIntyre, gamekeeper, Dalnaspidal; David Gow, labourer, Pitagowan; David Paterson, station master, Struan; John Stewart, Gamekeeper, Auchleeks and David MacIntyre, labourer, Struan:

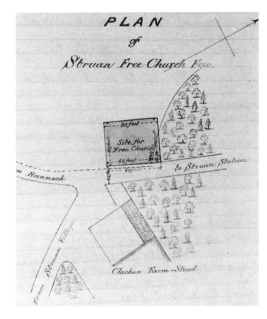

> All and whole that piece of ground upon which a building to be used as a place of worship by the congregation of the Free Church of Scotland at Struan extending to 17½ poles imperial, bounded on the north by Struan Wood on the east by the public road leading from Rannoch to Struan Station and on the south and west by the lands of Clachan.[26]

Struan Free Church, completed in 1879 and now a private house.

The church which was completed in 1879 across the road from Clachan of Struan farm had also a small vestry. A special pew was reserved for the Clachan residents and a block of seats was set aside for Calvine households, the largest settlement in the district. It continued as a church until the 1930s, after the uniting of the two denominations, when it closed and was used as a youth hostel. It was sold in the 1960s and converted to a private dwelling house.

References

1. *Memoir of Mrs Stewart Sandeman,* Barbour
2. PSAS   Volume 122
3. *Fasti*, Scott
4. TKSM
5. *Blair Atholl As It Was . . .*, Stuart
6. Ibid
7. Ibid
8. SRO CH 3 358/1
9. *Blair Atholl As It Was . . .*, Stuart
10. SRO CH 3 358/1
11. Church of Scotland, 121 George Street, Edinburgh
12. *Blair Atholl As It Was . . .*, Stuart
13. SRO CH 3 358/4
14. PSAS Volume 122
15. SRO CH 3 358/4
16. Ibid
17. SRO CH 3 358/2
18. Ibid
19. *Annals of the Free Church*, Ewing
20. Blair Atholl Session Minutes
21. BCCR Bundle 1152
22. *Blair Atholl As It Was . . .*, Stuart
23. BCCR Bundle 1723
24. *Blair Atholl As It Was . . .*, Stuart
25. SRO CH 3 358/1
26. BCCR AC

twelve

Burial Grounds and Gravestones

There are a number of private burial grounds and single gravestones in the Atholl area, quite separate from any church, some of which are well documented, while information on others is scarce.

Strathgarry Burial Ground

In a field to the south of Strathgarry Farm, near a stream which flows into the Garry, there is a small twentieth century enclosure which is the private family burial ground of the Stewarts of Strathgarry. Inside it are five headstones and an equal number of memorial plaques, one of which is to Kenneth Dugald Stewart, first baronet, who died in 1972.

In 1708 the Reverend Duncan Stewart, minister of Blair Atholl and Struan, became the first laird of Strathgarry when he bought the feu from the 1st Duke of Atholl. Alexander, his grandson, not only followed him into the ministry but also to Blair Atholl parish, where he held the post for forty years. His son, Duncan, became the fourth laird, having been ordained in 1773 and was granted Balquidder parish. Duncan's oldest son, Alexander, succeeded him and was the last Strathgarry laird to be buried in St Brides churchyard.

Private burial ground of the Stewarts of Strathgarry.

Bonskeid Burial Ground

The private burial ground of the Barbour family.

The private burial ground for the Barbour family of Glen Fincastle is located on a knoll in a clearing amongst mature trees a few hundred yards south of Bonskeid House and was created in 1887. It contains ten headstones from the nineteenth and twentieth centuries, together with two plaques attached to a rockface. The earliest headstone is to George Freeland Barbour, laird of Bonskeid, who died in 1887. His wife, Margaret, who wrote *Memoir of Mrs Margaret Sandeman*, died in 1892 and is also buried here. The two plaques bear the initials A H F B, standing for Alex Hugh Freeland Barbour and M N B for his wife, Margaret Nelson Barbour.

Chapelton of Fincastle

In Glen Fincastle, in the south-east corner of the parish, is the old settlement of Chapelton which has a stone-walled burial ground with ash and gean trees round its perimeter, a little way off the road through a field. There are eleven standing headstones and twenty flat ones from both the nineteenth and twentieth centuries, with one very indistinct inscription dated 1731. A stone in memory of Ida Janet Mackenzie, who died on 18 June 1907, bears the epitaph – "for 40 years faithfull and much loved friend and nurse in family of William McInroy of Lude". A modern stone bears memory to Matthew Dundas Stogdon, 3 October 1949 to 30 September 1993, who was killed in a car accident in Split, Croatia. He was an oil and water engineer whose family owned Balnald in Glen Fincastle and used it as a holiday cottage.

This burial ground was at one time in a detached part of the parish of Dull and according to Volume Four of *Fasti Ecclesiae Scoticanae*: "There is a burial ground near the head of Glenfinlas (sic) on a rocky mound called Chapelton, with ruins of a church in use till 1770". A reference to this church still being in use is recorded in the minutes of a meeting of the kirk session held in Blair Atholl on 22 March 1762, when Neil Stewart from Tombuie retracted his accusation that Robert Macdonald alias Caldel from Carrick "was guilty in stealing his sheeling" (ground grain). Neil admitted that what he had said was groundless and agreed that "the said confession should be read at the chappel of Fincastle after divine service there".

The graveyard at Chapelton of Fincastle.

Cladh Chille

Below the Bonskeid burial ground on flat land overlooking the River Tummel, is what has been described as an ancient Culdee burying place called Cladh Chille. It is now surrounded by a 1960s conifer plantation and is marked by a large, west-facing granite slab inscribed: "site of gateway to the old Culdee burial ground". This was put up by George Freeland Barbour in 1860 and apart from the enclosure wall itself there is no visible evidence of any remains inside.

The tradition goes that an ancient Culdee chapel once stood here and was associated with the Priest's Stone south of the river and in the nineteenth century a ring of thorn bushes grew within the enclosure walls. It is also said that when a new farm house was built nearby, the builders took some old grave stones to complete it, which thereafter gave rise to stories of supernatural happenings. Mrs Stewart Sandeman of Bonskeid related in her memoirs:

> While the farm-servants were at supper, stones came rattling down the chimney; and when the inmates went to bed, low moaning sounds were heard which would not let them sleep.

143

Colquhoun Burial Ground

About a mile further west along the Loch Tummel road there is a stoutly-built, castellated , square enclosure, now very overgrown with yew trees, overlooking the modern Clunie Hydro-Electric dam. This is the Colquhoun burial ground and has two memorial tablets in one of the walls. One is to the memory of Colonel Robert Stewart, the last Stewart laird of Fincastle, who died in 1822. The other is for Sir Robert Gilmore Colquhoun, KGB, the Fincastle laird who died in 1879, aged 67 years. Also there are his mother, Harriet, who died in 1836 and his daughter, Margaret Charlotte who died in 1838 aged 28 years.

The Stewart of Balchastle burial ground at Chapelton of Borenich.

Chapelton of Borenich

Above the shore of Loch Tummel, in a field west of Borenich farm is a small private burial ground with two headstones which belonged to Alexander Stewart, an Edinburgh lawyer. He was the youngest son of John Stewart, a farmer in nearby Balchastle and thereafter the innkeeper at the Diamond Inn, Bankfoot. He was buried in the graveyard in 1884, along with his son, John, who had been a cabinet maker in Edinburgh. The other stone is in memory of Simon Fraser, farmer in Tombuie, who died in 1831. There is also an iron cross with the name "Kirsty" on it.

Tressait

Not far from the Loch Tummel Hotel is the farmstead of Tressait, where, on the north side of An Tulach there was, (according to the late Dr Margaret Stewart, the archaeologist) a cemetery for unbaptised children. This spot is largely covered by clearance heaps of field stones and old rowan trees. There is now little to see, but a local recalled that in the 1950s, when he was a boy, a number of small turf mounds were clearly visible and he received a stern warning from his father never to dig in that area.

Location of the cemetry for unbaptised children.

Aldclune Grave Stone

Above the hamlet of Aldclune, near the Blair Atholl and Tenandry parish boundary there are the remains of a dyke marking the outline of a rectangular burial enclosure in a small clump of trees called the "Grave Wood". Inside this there are two flat stones within the footings of an old building. One, which is long and narrow is quite plain, while the second is incised C S 1760 with the outline of a Lochaber axe underneath. Christopher Bowstead suggested that CS stood for the initials of the sister of Walter Stewart of Orchil, one time minister of Kilmaveonaig but the presence of an axe would seem to indicate a man rather than a woman and might more likely be Walter's brother Charles.

Crawford Huie pointing out the gravestone above Aldclune.

Riecharlotte Grave Stone

Another solitary gravestone is situated two miles east of Shinagag, close to Allt na Leacainn Moire, the boundary between Blair Atholl and Moulin parishes. It is at the end of the estate track near Riecharlotte. This was a shieling named after Charlotte Robertson, "Lady Lude" who entertained Charles Edward Stuart at Lude House in 1745. Reicharlotte contains the substantial remains of at least ten buildings and a kiln. Early rental records reveal that the tenant in 1759 was Patrick Conacher, who paid £1.2.3 sterling a year and his contribution to the minister's stipend was 1/3d. In addition, he was obliged to provide services to the laird of stacking to dry and then transporting forty loads of peat to the laird's residence. He had the option of paying the cash equivalent of 2d a load but the records show he chose to carry the peat rather than pay the money. The upright stone with flat stone in front, bears witness to a coffin party approaching the shieling from Glen Brerachan, when a violent snowstorm caused the bearers to put down the coffin and scatter to safety. It was six weeks before they could return and rather than disturb the body it was decided that he should remain where he had already rested for so long, so they buried him on the spot.

The solitary grave marker, two miles east of Shinagag.

Morgan's Plaque

The ashes of a man who loved the hills and glens of Atholl were scattered on the hillside to the south of Shinagag in 1981. Barry John Morgan worked for a time in the Atholl Arms hotel and a metal plaque in his memory was fixed to a rockface with the inscription:

> BARRY JOHN MORGAN
> Aged 32 years
> Beloved son and brother
> Born 14th December 1948 Passed away 1st July 1981
> Because of his love for the peace and tranquility
> of these hills he requested that his ashes
> be scattered at this place
> FREE FOREVER

Memorial to Barry John Morgan, a mile south of Shinagag.

Tirinie

In the 1920s Lady Helen Stewart Murray, second daughter of the 7th Duke of Atholl, and her husband, Mr David Tod, a wealthy Edinburgh business man, bought the ground of Upper Tirinie in Glenfender, where they built a large country house and had a collection of fine furnishings and paintings by Scottish artists to grace their new home. Being well into middle age when they married, they had no children, so they left Tirnie House and grounds in trust as a:

> home for rest and change of air or holidays for such persons as the Endowment Trust may in their discretion select . . . said persons to be Scottish or of Scottish descent . . . with preference to be given to persons belonging to or connected with the clerical, legal, medical, surgical or artistic professions.

The notable list of trustees, including the Duke of Atholl, the Dean of the Faculty of Advocates, the President of the Royal Colleges of Physicians and Surgeons, the Presidents of the Royal Scottish Academy, along with the minister of Blair Atholl parish, ran the trust until the mid 1990s, with the great majority of those taking up the benefits being Church of Scotland ministers.

Mr Tod died in 1933 and was buried in a metal-railed enclosure in a small birch wood a few hundred yards west of the house. Lady Helen died in December of the following year and a report in the *Perthshire Advertiser* of 5 December 1934 described the funeral scene:

> Heavy snow showers swept the nearby Ben-y-Gloe mountains while the service was conducted in front of Tirinie House by Dr D. Lamont, Blair Atholl, in presence of a large and widely representative gathering. . . . The coffin – of unpolished oak, with silver mountings . . . was covered with an Atholl tartan plaid. . . . Thereafter the cortege preceded by Pipe Majors Alexander Stewart and Robert Irvine playing the "Slow Atholl March" wound its way to the little open space on the verge of the moorlands which is marked by a rough stone column, which had been selected by Lady Helen and Mr Tod themselves from the hillside, to form a headstone, in which had been fitted a copper plate

to bear their names. . . . A brief commital service was conducted at the grave, which was lined with hemlock spruce, after which a "lament" was played by Piper Peter Stewart.

The epitaph on the copper plaque, decorated with a Celtic cross and interlaced designs reads:

Sacred to the memory of
David Alexander Tod
Born 1859 Died 1933
And to his wife
Helen Stewart Murray
Daughter of John
7th Duke of Atholl
Born 1867 Died 1934
I will lift up mine eyes
Unto the hills
From whence cometh my
Help. My help cometh
From the Lord which
Made heaven and earth.

The headstone in the private burial enclosure in the grounds of Tirinie House.

Lady Evelyn Stewart Murray, the youngest of the 7th Duke's daughters, became an expert in two widely different areas. In her early twenties she devoted her energies to the study of Gaelic and the collecting of local Gaelic tales, her days being taken up with talking to the ordinary folk in north Perthshire. Later in life, when living in Belgium, she turned to collecting lace and doing fine needlework, of which exquisite examples are housed and displayed in Blair Castle. She died in July 1940 and had asked to be buried beside her sister Helen in the Tirinie burial ground. She requested a simple, private ceremony with no headstone and the only markers to her grave were two small rocks to the rear of the enclosure. In 1997, a simple brass plaque to her memory was added to the stone below that of her sister and brother-in-law.

Her brother, Lord James Stewart Murray described the funeral to a family member:

We laid her to rest next to Helen in the Tirinie cemetery amongst the hills and the heather which her heart had never forgotten. . . . The funeral was quite private. At the end Robert Irvine played a Gaelic melody on his pipes. . . .

In *Daughter of Atholl*, Sylvia Robertson, co-author of Lady Evelyn's biography, records having spoken many years later to the daughter of one of the pall bearers, who recalled her father speaking with some awe of a swan that had been seen that day on the small lochan below the burial ground, bringing to mind the old Highland belief that a swan was once a soul.

Appendix
The Reverend William Stewart

The Reverend William Stewart was born in May 1831 at Kinardochy and baptised in his father's house on 7 May 1831. He was educated at the village school in Foss and the universities of St Andrews and Edinburgh. On 18th March 1860 he preached at Struan as "a candidate for the mission there" and was immediately appointed, under the Blair Atholl and Struan parish minister, the Reverend Dr Alexander Irvine. He stayed in Struan schoolhouse with the teacher, Malcolm Grant and his two children and in the 1861 census his occupation was described as Assistant Minister of Blair Atholl. He emigrated to Canada three years later but his diary recounting his time as a minister in Argyll and north Perthshire has survived and reveals much about him as a minister and his social contacts with his family and the community.

22 April 1860.   Sabbath. Preached in Struan. Collection for the home mission scheme of the C. of Scotland. In the evening opened the Sabbath school.

2 May.   Wednesday. Left my father's house [Kinardochy] between 9 and 10 o'clock a.m. and came round by Trinafour where I visited the following families. Mrs McIntosh, John Kennedy the Smith, Robertson the wright, C— the taylor, and an old widow who was bedridden with whom I read and prayed and concerning whose recovery I had doubts. D. Campbell daughter and the merchant Robertson, and George R [Robertson], innkeeper. I also called at Mr Stewart Blairfettie. Arrived in Struan 1/4 before ten o' clock p.m.

5 May.   Saturday. Sat in the room writing till after dinner. Then went to Kindrochit park to commit what I had written. Paid a visit at the cottage. Doctored some bees.

8 June.   Friday. Left Struan 1/4 to 9 o' clock for Bruar Glen to fish. (The party Rev. I. Gilchrist, myself, Mr Grant, teacher and Mr Wm. Stewart Calvine) who drove us all up and down in his dog cart. Had a luncheon in Riuthdoch [Ruidhdorch, of which Dr Irvine the minister had a lease] Lodge. Got a pretty good day's sport.

19 June.   Tuesday. Left here after breakfast for the purpose of visiting some families and when I reached Calvin[e] I was told that there was a corpse in each of the two families I intended to visit. The intelligence struck me as a very wonderful thing indeed. Clunes and Dall were the two places I intended to visit.

20 June.   Wednesday. Attended a funeral at Clunes. Came down with the people to Calvin.

21 June.   Thursday. Attended the funeral of Alex. Robertson, Dall [Dalinturuaine].

2 July.   Monday. Left Struan at 1/4 before 8a.m. for Foss and when I got past Kynachan I arranged my fishing tackle and commenced operation and sad to say it was a long time before I caught any. But before I reached my father's house I managed to cheat some of them of the shallow pools.

4 July.   Wednesday. Spent a great part of the day looking at the sheepshearers and when the dinner hour came I heartily partook of a share of the sheepshearers' feast which was spread out on the unrivable carpet of nature. Clipped one sheep to keep me in remembrance of old lang syne. Had tea and a chat in the Braes [of Foss] in the evening.

13 July.   Friday. Studied all day. Had a short visit of his Reverence who left orders with me to prepare and go to K. Rannoch tomorrow to preach. I could very well stay at home as other preparations are rather pressing me too much.

14 July.   Saturday. Left about 7 o'clock a.m. for Kinloch Rannoch and arrived there at 1/4 past ten o' clock a.m. Preached in the church there English and Gaelic. Dined and tea in the Manse, after that a chase after the pony. Got it saddled and turned my back speedily on Kinloch.

15 July. Sabbath. Preached in Struan two sermons. In the evening went over to Strathtummel and preached a Gaelic sermon in the schoolroom there. Returned in the evening again to Struan, quite tired and fatigued.

12 August. Sabbath. Preached at Struan as usual to a very good congregation. (A bold attempt at offhand preaching in Gaelic, at times a little stiff and wandering from the subject.)

26 August. Sabbath. Preached at Blair to a large congregation. Among the rest were the Duke and Duchess of Atholl. Felt some shaky going into the pulpit but after getting a fair commencement made, I got more composed.

14 October. Sabbath. Preached English and Gaelic as usual. Got on shockingly bad at the Gaelic as I was interrupted in my speech by coughing. I endeavoured on its commencement to suppress it, which made it worse.

2 December. Sabbath. Was very much frightened at the appearance of the day when I first looked out. It was exceedingly boisterous. And when 10 o'clock came round I made my way toward church but found few if any before me. The bell was wrung and it too brought very few out of the shuttered nooks. Eight hearers was the sum in toto. Lectured them in Gaelic for about an hour and let them go home. I had to precent myself.

14 December. Friday. Studied the whole day. About dusk called at Kindrochit. Conducted the music and prayer meeting as usual, not with a very loving spirit as I was provoked seeing boys not behaving themselves in a comely manner. The sun was down before the wrath commenced and I resolved not to let the sun rise on my wrath.

10 February 1861. Sabbath. Preached at Struan English and Gaelic to a very large congregation, about 110 present. Conducted the Sabbath school in the evening.

13 February. Wednesday. Had a walk before dinner along the river side, my general place of resort at present when I am anxious to have a secluded spot where I will not be heard though speaking aloud. About 4 o'clock p.m. left for Strathtummel. Visited there the old wright with whom I read and prayed. Preached in the schoolroom to a good meeting. Returned about 1/2 past ten. Felt the road to be very slippery. Favoured the birds on the top of the hill with some hymns and psalms which kept me from wearying while pacing slowly across the rugged moor.

14 July. Sabbath. Preached at Struan in the English from Isaiah 27.13 and in Gaelic I Kings 18.21. Congregation pretty good but rather Englified as many of them left at the end of the English service:

Some folks pretend no Gaelic they understand
As English is gaining ground in our Highland land
And fair ones view Gaelic as a vulgar tongue -
aimed merely to twist the lips to wrong...

9 October. Wednesday. Attended a funeral from Dalnameen (a child of Crerar). Called at Tomchitchen, at the post and shop and while there saw the Queen passing. [Queen Victoria was travelling from Dalwhinnie to Blair Castle and then through Glen Tilt to Balmoral.]

1 December. Sabbath. Preached at Blair, E. & G. Left at 4 p.m. again for 'Tomcraggach where I opened the Sabbath school and gave a Gaelic sermon. Had the Minister's dog cart up and down. Returned to Struan about 9 p.m.

1 April 1862. Tuesday. Went down to Pitagowan to examine the school with Dr Irvine. Paid a visit to the navvies at their work. [Construction of the Perth- Inverness railway.]

8 October. Wednesday. Went to the post office in the evening and took a walk down to inspect the railway a good piece.

9 October. Thursday. Studied the whole day till 5 o' clock when I went down to Bruar to see a reaping machine at work.

30 October. Thursday. Rode up to Dalnacardoch where I made a call. Called at the Toll, at J. McLachlan's house. Spoke to Mr Grieve the railway contractor about a schoolhouse which he was willing to grant.

9 November. Sabbath. Preached a Gaelic sermon at Tummelbridge. Dr Irvine at Struan. The day very stormy and congregation very small. Returned to Kinardochy in the evening. Towards evening the snow commenced to lay thick upon the ground.

28 December. Sabbath. Left Struan at 10 o' clock with the intention of preaching at Blair. Went down on the South side of the river and when I reached the three boats could not get across by any of them. Therefore I was obliged to return home without having had an opportunity of preaching at all. Felt very much disappointed.

9 January 1863. Friday. Visited [a sick] tinker again and gave him a line with a view to get some relief of the parish for a few days.

10 March. Tuesday. Was present at the laying of the foundation stone of the Railway Bridge across the Garry. Kept no particular holiday to show my loyalty to the future King.

16 April. Thursday. Left Struan at 1/2 past 7 in the morning. Breakfasted in the manse. Went down to Pitlochry after that and underwent some trials there previous to ordination. Got ordination from the presbytery of Dunkeld. Dined with the Presbytery in the Hotel again. Returned with Dr Irvine to the Manse of Blair and made my way on foot again the best way I could to Struan. Very tired and sleepy and low in spirits.

26 April. Sabbath. Preached at Struan English and Gaelic. Took farewell of the congregation amid sobbings and tears.

24 May. Sabbath. Heard Mr McKellar preach in Foss. It was the last preaching I heard in Scotland.

31 May. Sabbath. On board the R. M. S. *Africa* for Halifax.

Extracts from *The Life of the Reverend William I Stewart* Printed privately 1998. Transcribed and edited by Katherine Stewart Paine McIntyre, Houston, Texas.

Glossary

Bands	Door hinges
Beamfill	Fill the space between the wall plate and the roof
Birlieman	An arbiter or umpire in local matters
Blewwood	Blown timber
Boll	Volumetric grain measure equivalent to 140 lb (63.5kg) of ground oats
Chalder	Equivalent to 16 bolls
Cleek	Hook
Cottar	Holder of a small piece of land, held in return for services, usually labouring.
Cuples	Pair of rafters forming a V-shaped roof support
Crook	Iron hook on which a door or gate is hung
Cuir	Spiritual charge
Dale	Deal, board of standard length
Devot, Divot	Turf, sod
Ell	Measure of length, the Scottish ell being about 37 inches (94 cm)
Fall	Measure of 6 square ells
Feal	Turf used for building and roofing
Fewal	Fuel, often peat
Firlot	Fourth part of a boll
Foggage	Second crop of grass after hay
Garron nail	Large nail or spike
Gavel	Gable
Head-dyke	Wall which separated arable and meadow ground from hill pasture
Isle	Aisle, passage between pews
Kailyard	Kitchen garden
Laigh floor	Ground Floor
Loft	Gallery
Moss	Boggy place where peat was dug
Multure	Duty consisting of a proportion of grain ground, exacted by the mill proprietor
Office house	Outbuilding or workshop
Paten	Shallow dish for Communion bread
Pendicle	Small portion of land allotted by a farmer to his labourers and servants
Plenshion	Flooring nail
Press	Large cupboard, often built into a recess in a wall
Quire	Choir
Rygan Stones	Stones for the ridge of a roof
Rybets	Dressed stones at the side of windows and doors
Rood	An area of 36 square ells of masonry or slatework
Shieling	Grazing ground and bothies used in summer, usually in the mountains
Silver Dewtie	Money payment due to a feudal superior
Skaillie/Skeillie	Slates
Skew	A stone forming part of the coping of the sloping part of a gable
Sneck	Latch or catch of a door
Teind silver	Money paid as teind (tenth part) in lieu of goods
Torus	A large moulding
Vassal	Holder of heritable property in feu from a superior
Vent	Fireplace
Walk Miln	Fulling mill for soaking, beating and shrinking cloth
Winning	Quarrying stones
Wright	Carpenter or joiner

Bibliography

Primary Sources

Charter Room, Blair Castle
Atholl Chartularies

Volume I 1706-1724; Untitled Volume – Document dated 1.7.1878

Trunks

9   Contracts of feus, sasines and charters
29   Correspondence 1579-1698
33   Duke v Struan Correspondence, Struan Church
45   Correspondence 1699-1720
46   Correspondence 1721-1744
48   Correspondence 1800-1810
54   Correspondence 1770-1774
59   Correspondence 1794-1799
65   Correspondence 1775-1793
68   Correspondence 1811-1824
69   Correspondence 1825-1830

Bundles

224   Miscellaneous papers including correspondence relating to Blair Glebe and church sittings, Old Blair church and burial ground
1127 Details of various properties on the Atholl estate
1152 Petition by Struan congregation for a site to build a church, 1844
1226 Papers relating to ecclesiastical affairs 1819-1868
1227 Papers relating to ecclesiastical affairs 1820-1830, to parish of Blair and Struan, division of seats and fabric of Blair church and manse
1228 Papers relating to ecclesiastical affairs 1800-1830; proposed suppression of Struan church
1240 State of teinds in the parish for 1833, 1834 and stipends 1757, 1833. Legal opinion concerning case brought by Rev John Stewart against his heritors
1285 Letters to Fred Graham on parochial matters c 1826 including building part of Blair manse and division of seats in Blair church
1723 19th century church papers including petition to duke by Free Church congregation at Struan for a site to build a church
7.417 Rentals

Maps and Plans

A1   Plan of Blair in Atholl, Forest of Tarff, Benechrombie in Perthshire, James Stobie, 1780
A2   Ordnance Survey, First Edition 25", Perthshire
A7   A General Map of Scotland and Islands, James Dorret, 1750
A 13 Plan of Atholl House, Gardens, Parks and Inclosures, James Dorret 1758

B5   A Plan for Blair in Atholl by Chas Esplen from Thomas Winters 1744

D.5.1   Plan of the Castle Gardens Plantations, etc. of Blair in Atholl . . . John Tinney, 1744

D.5.14 Plan of the Common of Glentilt as Divided, David Buist, 1808

D.5.19 Draft of the Barony and Lands of Lude as presently possessed to the South and East of Water of Tilt, 1790

D.5.41 Plan of Strowan, undated

Ordnance Survey Second Edition 6" Perthshire, 1900

Legal Papers

Map of "Shierglass" island contained in document on "Fishing Case" dispute: McInroy of Shierglass v Duke of Atholl, 1864

Scottish Record Office
Dunkeld Presbytery Minutes

CH 2	106/3	1712-1717
	106/4	1717-1724
	106/5	1724-1731
	106/6	1731-1746
	106/7	1746-1754
	106/10	1782-1793
	106/13	1815-1823
	106/14	1823-1829
	106/15	1829-1835
	106/16	1835-1845
	106/17	1845-1863
	106/18	1863-1885

Blair Atholl and Struan Free Church Minutes

CH 3	358/1	Minutes	1844-1886
	358/2	Deacons Court Minutes	1876-1898
	358//4	Seat Letting Book	1857-1900

Blair Atholl and Struan Kirk Session Minutes

CH 2	430/1	1718-1723
	430/2	1741-1759
	430/3	1759-1780
	430/6	1763-1796
	430/7	1796-1815
	430/8	1815-1828

Robertson of Lude Papers

GD 132   730/1, 731, 797/1

Baron Court of Lude Papers

GD 50   159

Miscellaneous Primary Sources

A K Bell Library, Perth, Archaeological Notes of the late Dr Margaret Stewart.

Sir Robin Barbour, Old Fincastle, Tenandry Kirk Session Minutes.

Church of Scotland, 121 George Street, Edinburgh, Church Archives.

Reverend Roger Devonshire, Pitlochry, Holy Trinity Church Pitlochry Records.

Mrs Lavinia Gordon, Lude, Kilmaveonaig Church Records.

Major W G Gordon, Lude House, Plan of Lude Estate, 1820.

Mrs K. Patterson, St Andrews, Notes on Glenfender Inhabitants.

James Irvine Robertson, Aberfeldy, Correspondence of the Rev. Dr Alexander Irvine, on Struan suppression and other matters.

Sebastian Thewes, Strathgarry House, Strathgarry Estate Papers.

Secondary Sources

Anderson, Arthur, *The Bell of St Fillan of Struan in Athole*, Proceedings of the Society of Antiquaries of Scotland, Volume XIII. 1879

Anderson, Jane, ed. *Chronicles of the Atholl and Tullibardine Families*, Volume 6, 1991

Anderson, John, *Guide to the Highlands*, 1870

Atholl, 7th Duke of, *Chronicles of the Atholl and Tullibardine Families*, Vols 1, 4, 5, 1908

Barbour, Margaret, *A Short History of Tenandry Kirk 1836-1986*

Barbour, Margaret, *Memoir of Mrs Stewart Sandeman of Bonskeid and Springland*, 1883

Bell, Thomas, ed. *Records of the Meeting of the Excise of Alford*, New Spalding Club, 1897

Black Book of Taymouth, reprint, Kilchurn Heritage, 1993

Bowstead, Rev. C I K, *Facts and Fancies Linked With Folklore About Kilmaveonaig* c.1915

Cameron, Rev Donald, *Sermon* from Clan Donnachaidh Society Annual Service, as reprinted in the 1955 Clan Donnachaidh Annual.

Clouson, R W M, *The Bells of Perthshire*, Proceedings of the Society of Antiquaries of Scotland, Volume 122, 1992.

Donaldson, Gordon, *Accounts of the Collectors of Thirds of Benefices*, Scottish History Society, Third Series, 1949.

Donaldson, Gordon, *Scotland, Church and Nation through Sixteen Centuries,* 1960

Ewing, Rev. William, ed. *Annals of the Free Church of Scotland*, Volume 2, 1914

Galbraith, Dr J J, *The Parish in Highland History*, Transactions of the Gaelic Society of Inverness, Volume XXXVIII, 1937-1941.

Glasgow Citizen, 27 September 1844.

Gow, James Mackintosh, *Holiday Notes in Atholl, Perthshire*, Proceedings of the Society of Antiquaries of Scotland, Volume XXIV, 1889-1890.

Hannay, Robert K, ed. *Rentale Dunkeldense*, Scottish History Society, Second Series, 1915.

Haws, Charles, H, *Scottish Parish Clergy at the Reformation 1540-1574*, Scottish Record Society, 1972.

Hunter, John, *The Diocese and Presbytery of Dunkeld, 1647-1689*, Volume II, 1917.

Kerr, John, *East by Tilt*, Transactions of the Gaelic Society of Inverness, Volume LIV, 1984-1986.

Kerr, John, *Queen Victoria's Scottish Diaries*, 1992

Laing, David, ed. *Register of Ministers and Readers in the Kirk of Scotland*, from the Book of the Assignation of Stipends, Wodrow Society Miscellany, Volume I, 1844.

Leneman, Leah, *Living in Atholl 1685-1785*, 1986.

MacLagan, Rev. James, *Parishes of Blair-Atholl and Strowan*, in the Statistical Account of Scotland, 1792.

Meek, Donald E, *The Independent and Baptist Churches of Highland Perthshire and Strathspey*, Transactions of the Gaelic Society of Inverness, Volume LVI, 1988-1990.

Moulin and Tenandry Parish Magazine, September 1902.

Munro, Dr Jean, *Robertson Hatchments at Kilmaveonaig*, Clan Donnachaidh Annual, 1960.

Perthshire Advertiser, 5 December 1934.

Rees, Jack, *The Wood Burns away but the Fire goes on for ever*, 1983.

Robertson, J A, *Comitatus de Atholia, The Earldom of Atholl, Its Boundaries Stated*, 1860.

Robertson, Sylvia and Young, Patricia, *Daughter of Atholl, Lady Evelyn Stewart-Murray 1868-1940*, 1996

Scots Magazine, 1749

Scott, Hew, *Fasti Ecclesiae Scoticanae*, Synods of Argyll and of Perth and Stirling, Volume 4, 1915.

Shennan, Hay, *Boundaries of Counties and Parishes in Scotland*, 1892.

Smith, Alexander, *A Quest for an Ancestor*, 1989.

Stewart, Rev. John, *Parish of Blair-Atholl*, in the New Statistical Account of Scotland, 1845.

Stuart, Rev. Atholl, *Blair Atholl as it Was and Is. . .* 1857

Surtees, Virginia, *Charlotte Canning*, 1975.

Watson, William J, *The History of the Celtic Place-Names of Scotland*, 1926.

Wilkie, James, *St Bride*, 1913.

Wilson, Daniel, *Primitive Scottish Bells*, Proceedings of the Society of Antiquaries of Scotland, Volume I.

Index

John Kerr on the Errochty bridge in front of Struan Church.

John Kerr's interest in Atholl dates back to 1960, when a chance conversation with the late Alec MacRae, Blair Atholl garage proprietor and local historian further stirred an existing interest in old roads and communications. He became a member of the Gaelic Society of Inverness in 1968, to which he has since contributed seven papers. He was made an FSA (Scot) in 1974 and in 1984 established "The Atholl Experience", an ever-changing historical exhibition supported by twinscreen slide lectures. His first book, *Highland Highways*, was published in 1991 and *Church and Social History of Atholl* is his fifth on Atholl-based subject matters. John Kerr lives with his wife in Old Struan and has a grown up family with seven grandchildren.

Back cover: Struan Celtic Bell
by courtesy of Perth Museum and Art Gallery

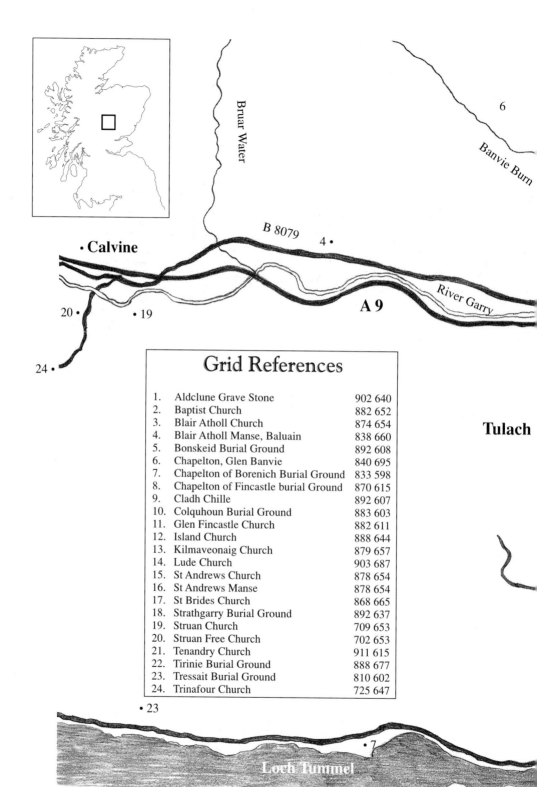

Bruar Water

6

Banvie Burn

B 8079   4 •

• Calvine

River Garry

20 •   • 19   A 9

24 •

Grid References

1.	Aldclune Grave Stone	902 640
2.	Baptist Church	882 652
3.	Blair Atholl Church	874 654
4.	Blair Atholl Manse, Baluain	838 660
5.	Bonskeid Burial Ground	892 608
6.	Chapelton, Glen Banvie	840 695
7.	Chapelton of Borenich Burial Ground	833 598
8.	Chapelton of Fincastle burial Ground	870 615
9.	Cladh Chille	892 607
10.	Colquhoun Burial Ground	883 603
11.	Glen Fincastle Church	882 611
12.	Island Church	888 644
13.	Kilmaveonaig Church	879 657
14.	Lude Church	903 687
15.	St Andrews Church	878 654
16.	St Andrews Manse	878 654
17.	St Brides Church	868 665
18.	Strathgarry Burial Ground	892 637
19.	Struan Church	709 653
20.	Struan Free Church	702 653
21.	Tenandry Church	911 615
22.	Tirinie Burial Ground	888 677
23.	Tressait Burial Ground	810 602
24.	Trinafour Church	725 647

Tulach

• 23

• 7

Loch Tummel